# JEZEBEL IN OUR MIDST

The Making of a Prophet

## by Harriet McGowan

D1490529

Copyright © 2007 by Harriet McGowan

*Jezebel In Our Midst*
*The Making of a Prophet*
by Harriet McGowan

Printed in the United States of America

ISBN 978-1-60477-311-8

All rights reserved solely by the author. The author guarantees all contents are original and do not infringe upon the legal rights of any other person or work. No part of this book may be reproduced in any form without the permission of the author. The views expressed in this book are not necessarily those of the publisher.

Unless otherwise indicated, Bible quotations are taken from the King James Version of the Bible.

First Printing 2007

www.xulonpress.com

# TABLE OF CONTENTS

# CHAPTER 1—The Message

Initially the author's purpose was to expose Jezebel and to warn others of this destructive force. But after some time, it became obvious that this was negative and narrow in scope and that the Lord had much greater intentions. His focus was not on Jezebel, but on raising a company of Elijahs in preparation for the end times.

We all know that His ways are higher than ours, and this conflict with Jezebel could not be a better example. Who would think that He would allow this ambassador of hell to get such a foothold in a congregation? But who would imagine that He would make a prince out of Joseph by locking him in a dungeon for years? Through destruction and desperation, God whittled this young man into a world leader because he learned to lean on his maker and obtained wisdom in exchange.

That is the message of this book. The Lord is using Jezebel to raise up mature saints who have control of their vessels and who know how to operate successfully in the Spirit. They also know the heart of the Father toward the wayward that oppose them and have been conditioned to respond in a loving and godly manner demonstrating more and more of Christ's character. They know the meaning of "having done all to stand, stand" and unflinchingly wait for the salvation of God. But most importantly, they know the Father. They are worshippers as well as warriors. The Lord has enabled them to reach a level of prayer that changes things because they know how to seek Him with all their hearts. This company of believers is sold out to the Lord and is desirous that He receive the glory.

> *There is a pressure like none other that comes from Jezebel, and **that's** what the Lord is after.*

*Jezebel in Our Midst* demonstrates how the Lord can maneuver a life until these traits become evident. While many books expose the workings of Jezebel and explain how to recognize this principality, the blueprint for its expulsion is never made clear. Could it be the Lord doesn't want it done away with until He's completed His work in our lives? There is a pressure like none other that comes from Jezebel, and *that* is what the Lord is after. He is creating a new work in our lives. Thousands of years ago, fossil fuels and diamonds were created in the earth through pressure and today are considered a sign of wealth.

Elijah was a mighty man of God, so you can imagine that the Lord may have to use some extraordinary measures to mold similar character in us. Many try to war their way out of this mess, but the Lord has a much higher plan involving an extended spin on the potter's wheel. There are literally times when we will be smashed to nothing and the process will begin all over. Without this knowledge, people will run. Suffering is not a popular topic because much emphasis is put on prosperity today, but if you're after the higher things of God, you'll stay the course. His grace enables us to finish, and with rewards along the way. He knows our temperaments and how much pressure we can handle. In the end, there will be no regret, only satisfaction—a sign of His handiwork!

# CHAPTER 2—Jezebel in the Midst

At first glance, the spirit of Jezebel appears to be an isolated instance, but in reality, it is evident in many arenas. After the Lord has used Jezebel to do a work in a local body of Christ, it will be necessary *eventually* to rout this enemy from the midst.

Before going any further, it is important to emphasize that the Lord is in complete control. The enemy may start out with a plan of destruction, but the Lord can work it for our good. He will perfect, establish, strengthen, and settle us while the enemy is attempting to do a crushing. In effect, the Lord uses Satan as a tool to create His character in us. He perfects us, teaches our hands to war, instructs us in His ways, and draws us even closer to His side. No wonder the Word says the Lord sits in the heavenlies and laughs at the enemy.

The Word of God says that He gives us travail that we might be exercised by it. It makes us strong.

We learn about the enemy's camp and his tactics, but most of all, we learn about the ways of the Lord because we can't get out of Jezebel's web without asking for His help. All the while, He draws us into His presence, but He does not give us the information we need until we conform to His ways and His Word. Little by little, we start to change in character and gain His likeness and image. This uncomfortable situation with Jezebel is not permanent, but it may require a great deal of endurance and trust. In the end, we will be in possession of a grateful heart.

The Lord desires to do much in our lives, but there are few who will allow Him to fully complete His work. His ways are far different from ours, and His time frame truly seems to be eternal. As a result, saints give up long before they are finished. Many wonder how a loving God could take His children through such arduous paths. If only we would trust and obey Him, we would see a truly beautiful work at the end, as well as a fulfillment of His promises.

It breaks the heart of the Lord when His children will not yield fully to Him. He chooses different, and often painful, means to work something beautiful in our lives. If we hold steady, we will marvel at the wonderful creation unobtainable on an easier path.

**BEGINNING STAGES**

In the early stages of development, a Jezebelite, someone with a spirit of Jezebel, appears very similar to an average person. Many of us have had to use cajoling, manipulation, and some control in our lives. Parents have to operate this way to coax their children to do things that they do not want to do. Teachers have to motivate students to learn. Supervisors have to find ways to get the most work out of the labor force, and pastors have to apply pressure to get people on the right track. None of this is new, nor is it wrong, but the difference between these examples and someone operating out of a Jezebel spirit is *motive*. The examples above are for the benefit of the people involved, not for the parent, teacher, and so forth.

The motive of Jezebelites, however, is entirely different. They may operate in the same manner as the examples above, but their goal is to achieve something for themselves. Jezebelites are capable of feigning concern, friendship, or even affection in order to obtain more beneficial positions. At one time, they may have learned to operate as leaders for the benefit of others, but the enemy gained a foothold and gradually they crossed that fine line. What was once done out of love and concern is now a deceptive means for personal gain and must be called manipulation and control.

*If you're judgmental, it will come from your soul, but, if you're discerning, it will come from your spirit.*

You might wonder, *How can anyone know the motive of someone else's heart?* Certainly you can't go around being suspicious of everyone. Just be aware that these things *can* happen, so when the Holy Spirit makes your spirit feel uneasy about someone, don't regard it as impossible or judgmental. If you're judgmental, it will come from your soul, and you might end up gossiping; but if you're discerning, it will come from your spirit, and hopefully you'll pray.

Most of all, anyone is capable of slipping into wrong motives, including this author. This doesn't happen to just unsavory or seedy-looking characters. It can happen to someone who has lived an exemplary life, but whom the enemy hits with a terrible temptation. What a service we would be doing for that individual if we lifted him or her up in prayer and defeated the enemy's destructive plan!

One of two things can happen at this point. The first example involves individuals who get ahead of the Lord and try to make His will happen through manipulation and control rather than trusting the Lord for His timing. The second example includes those who work apart from the Lord's will and seek to carry out their own plans. We may all do this to some extent, and the Lord keeps working with us until we come around. However, when people continue to resist the turning of the Lord, then they are demanding their way. This is rebellion, and it is likened unto witchcraft in Scripture. While this is not necessarily a spirit of Jezebel, it is an individual operating in sorcery and witchcraft. If left unchecked for a considerable amount of time, it can develop into such, however.

It is important to note here that a person may be totally unaware, at first, that he or she is housing this principality. It could be a simple case of an individual with an exorbitant desire. Even if it is a perfectly respectable thing, it can be out of proportion to the person's love for the Lord and will eventually evolve into sin. The enemy can gain entrance if the person continues in this vein and the sin goes unchecked. That is why it is so important to yield to the Lord and allow Him to search our hearts frequently.

Once He has nudged us numerous times and we have hardened our hearts, then the trouble begins. It is at this point that the enemy can take ground and proceed with his plan.

When our desires become more important than the will of the Lord, the enemy is able to ride the wave of our wrong desires and gain entrance to operate in the church. As you can see, this can be a slow and lengthy process at first, but groundwork is important in anyone's camp. As the enemy rides on the wave of this person's desires, he has his own agenda. He will make sure that the plans and needs of this individual are fulfilled, falsely leading the person to believe that the Lord is answering his or her prayers. In actuality, it is the enemy at work, weaving his own web to ruin the pastor and the church involved.

These spirits reside in individuals who are unsaved or in the soul realm of the saved. They aren't fussy, and oftentimes the people have no idea that they are acting in league with the enemy. Previous generations can pass along these spirits, or they can be acquired through close or constant association.

If this spirit has been spiritually inherited, it can lie dormant for years and not manifest itself until a situation involving competition and strife comes into play. If jealousy and envy are left unchecked, they can actually be the driving force behind the scene.

The spirit of Jezebel is a highly organized principality that can work undetected by the human eye. The only outward manifestation might be a great deal of unexplained trouble for some individuals. People in leadership often find themselves out the door and wonder how it ever happened.

## LATER STAGES

Individuals who have contracted this Jezebel spirit can "grow spiritually" within that evil gifting. As their plans are threatened, this spirit will begin to operate. The more the individuals yield to controlling tendencies, the more they open themselves up to this demonic force. It may start out in a small measure that is hardly perceptible, yet it will register as unsettling in your spirit.

As Christians yield to righteousness, so too will they demonstrate more of the fruits of the Holy Spirit. As a result, the Lord will be able to work through and operate out of them in a greater measure. The same thing is true in the enemy's camp. Those who yield to jealousy or control will become more proficient in that area of sin, and the enemy will be able to use them to a greater degree. As their sphere of control increases, the power of their wrong prayer increases. Since this is a very deceptive principality, the veil that hides the clandestine work becomes even more effective too.

# CHARACTERISTICS OF JEZEBEL IN THE MIDST

People afflicted with these spirits are proud and controlling. If they are saved, the spirit can come from a strong desire that has overshadowed their love for the Lord. This, of course, is known as idolatry, a trait attributed to the historical Jezebel.

One of the more obvious characteristics of individuals suffering from this spiritual malady is an air of superiority. They seem to exude confidence to such a degree that listeners will probably not consider them to be in error. Subsequently, the listeners begin to doubt their own abilities, and they begin to feel inferior. Actually, they're looking at the spirit of intimidation.

You might think that you would never fall prey to such a tool of the enemy. However, persons driven by this spirit can disarm you with their winning personalities. They may often appear to be very sweet — even soft and velvety to the point that you consider yourself wicked indeed to even suspect them of foul play. This is how victims first come under the spell of Jezebel. When someone is exceedingly nice, it is often a means of manipulation — another key to identification.

Oddly enough, when this prince controls them, they may appear very religious and may even have a false humility and holiness. When they speak, it can be with great fervor for the Lord. They want people to believe that their relationship is much closer with the Lord than it really is. They may even go so far as to imply that God speaks face-to-face with them, thus filling others with awe and eliminating the prospect of any challengers.

When pastors have been beguiled, they often endorse the actions of the person in question. This, by the way, is very possible, since the pastor is usually the first and primary target to win over. It may take time and patience, but these people are opportunists filled with plots and plans. Just as the Lord will open doors for His children, so too will the enemy open doors for someone under his employ.

When Jezebelites are in positions of leadership, they will have remarkable showmanship that can often be mistaken for a move of the Holy Spirit. People who have this Jezebel spirit cannot tolerate standing in someone else's shadow. The need to lead can be so strong that they will actually manipulate the proceedings through various means. They seek supremacy and crave the limelight, for being in control is addictive to those operating out of a Jezebel spirit.

This desire to dominate a service can result in actual blocks, bindings, and incapacitations going on in the spirit realm over various individuals. At this point, intimidation begins to operate over the congregation, and as a result, the people are greatly hampered in their ability to bring forth that which the Lord has given them. This is especially the case if many in the body are new at moving in the Holy Spirit.

Does this sound impossible? Saved individuals with a Jezebel spirit love something *more* than they love the Lord, yet they profess through worship or preaching that He is the most important thing in their lives. When they state this, it doesn't ring true in the spirit. That's why it's important to be alert and to rely on the Holy Spirit. Their lives are lies. They are going through the motions, but they stopped obeying the Lord a long time ago. They know the lingo and the routine, and they look good!

*Beware if someone is carrying on like Moses, but there's no fragrance of the Lord.*

Look for the fragrance of the Lord in a person's life. If someone is carrying on like Moses yet there is no fragrance, then there could be a false spirit involved. People who genuinely love the Lord carry the fragrance of the Lord in varying degrees, and it comes out in their worship and preaching. With a Jezebelite, the words might be the same, but the fragrance of the Lord is missing. There is no beauty or drawing of the Lord. The atmosphere is flat and dry.

# CHAPTER 3 — Targets

With Jezebel in your midst, all desire to begin a new work or complete a work in progress will be greatly diminished. For example, an attempt at witnessing can result in absolutely no response despite the fact that much prayer and preparation have gone forth by seasoned workers. One young evangelist made a great analogy while attempting to drink a bottle of Gatorade. He noticed that a seal was under the cap. He exclaimed, "That's it! That's exactly what our witnessing was like today. We had everything we needed—prayer, the Word, experience—yet it was just like the juice in this bottle; it was blocked and nothing came forth." The prayers of a Jezebelite were in effect and needed to be bound.

In addition, intercessory meetings can dwindle to virtually nothing and be riddled with strife and confusion. Those operating with the Jezebel spirit can pray and cause various individuals to be tied up or blocked during the course of a meeting if saints are unaware. Jezebelites who know the realm of intercession are comparable to a lawman gone bad. They know how to operate in the spirit realm, and the same tactics they previously used against the enemy are now being waged against the saints whom *they* consider to be deceived.

Church growth can be stifled for years if this principality is left unchecked. The entire church can be stalled indefinitely with no apparent or explainable reason. This can be due to Jezebel, Python, and Leviathan at work within a church. They have the ability to block, bind, and generally incapacitate the forward motion of a church without the knowledge of the pastor or the board members. This is very possible if the members of the congregation are ignorant of the enemy's devices or do not inquire of the Lord concerning his infiltration.

When the spirit of Jezebel is in operation, private prayer can also be a real chore. Jezebel's cohorts actually stand with the intent of blocking a person's prayer. It is a weird sensation that makes you feel as though you are not really praying and borders on being surreal in nature. Prayer and intercession are greatly hampered, and it is necessary to punch a hole in the atmosphere surrounding you in order to reach the throne. It can be done, but it certainly takes away the joy of sitting down with the Lord in prayer. In order to break through, it is necessary to bind any blocks and incapacitations put in place by the enemy.

Those operating in conjunction with a Jezebel spirit can actually cut you from the Lord during prayer or worship. In either case, when you try to communicate with the Lord, you realize that there simply is no connection. You are not receiving any feedback in your spirit. It is as if you were talking on the phone with a friend and suddenly realized that you'd been disconnected. It can be remedied by simply binding any cutting prayers and any spirits that bind, block, or incapacitate your praise and worship. It may or may not be a case of someone deliberately praying and asking the Lord to separate you from Him, but prayers with wrong intentions or wrong heart attitudes on the part of Jezebelites can give the enemy license to hinder or obstruct your progress.

Another interesting aspect of a Jezebel spirit is the amount of psychic manipulation that takes place. When a Jezebelite targets individuals or intercessors, their minds can be greatly afflicted with vain imaginations, distractions, and confusion. Their thought processes can be hampered in varying degrees, ranging from mild to extreme interference involving the simplest of thought patterns. According to Jonas Clark in his book entitled *Exposing Spiritual Witchcraft*, this is a result of witchcraft in operation. There is definitely a strain on the brain, and maintaining an intelligent conversation is almost impossible. Not only is it difficult to carry on daily activities when mind control and sorcery are in operation, but decision-making within a church can suffer wrong turns and enable the enemy to maneuver his people into profitable positions.

*Spiritual Warfare* by Richard Ing states that people can feel like there are bands on their heads, and in actuality, that exists in the spirit realm. It is also possible that there are tentacles in the form of a giant squid wrapped around a person. In the natural, this animal can have a span of forty feet and still manage to reduce itself and hide undetected at the bottom of the sea, and so it is in the spirit world.

Similarly, it is entirely possible for a mature Jezebelite to control the preaching of a service, especially if the individual ministering is undiscerning or is not aware of Jezebel's capabilities. It is amazing to witness a speaker who goes forth with the intent of exposing this spirit within the church and then watch that person get turned around and be manipulated instead. This can be done because persons housing a Jezebel spirit can have the ability to project thoughts to others. They can plant wrong perceptions, suspicions, and so forth. It's just part of their makeup.

Also, if a Jezebelite has overcome the pastor, and the intercessors are not successful in binding up this prince, it is possible for the pastor to become the mouthpiece for the Jezebelite and convey that attitude through sorcery and witchcraft. As a result, various individuals in the congregation are repeatedly bruised, and trouble arises within the church. The enemy's intent is to conquer and divide by weeding out anyone who does not come under the Jezebelite's control.

It is interesting to note that many of the spiritual enemies comprised within this Jezebel spirit are deft at concealing themselves. Obfuscation or the ability to confuse, darken, or conceal a matter is often employed when this group of spirits is involved. It is possible for the enemy to hide completely if this particular spirit is in operation. It is through this spirit that the principality of Jezebel can successfully remain undetected by most of a congregation.

In addition, it is important to recognize some of the enemy's tricks. They do not pose a real threat and can be dodged with a little wisdom. For instance, a Jezebelite can act sweetly and at the same time send a totally different message in the spirit. Generally, others involved will not pick up this act of duplicity unless they flow well in discernment. To the outward eye, the behavior of the host can be almost exemplary, yet simultaneously the Jezebelite can be throwing his or her spirit at you, knowing full well that as an intercessor, you are capable of picking this up. This can be difficult at first, because now you are picking up some hateful darts. Be careful. It's so easy to respond improperly when you know that you're right and the other person is wrong, but rein in your emotions because *it is a trap!*

If you have the misfortune of taking the bait set by the enemy, you will find yourself guilty of answering in anger, and the Jezebelite will look like the victim of an unprovoked attack! Cute little tactic, wouldn't you say?

If you have any junk in your heart toward this individual, it will come out at this time and you will look like the culprit. God works His character in your life one way or another. At first glance, it appears to be unfair that the Lord would allow someone to get away with this. However, if you are on the receiving end, it will force you to learn how to control your emotions and ensure that your heart is free from resentment. It takes just a few instances of responding inappropriately and looking like the guilty party to learn how to maintain your composure and respond in love.

It is important to interject and present this information in a balanced manner. Please keep in mind that while the spirit of Jezebel can cause damage within a church, the Lord is in control. He is doing a work in the people involved, and when the time comes for their release from captivity, Jezebel will be no match for the Lord. He can easily turn the tables and set the camp in order.

## FOLLOWERS OF JEZEBEL

One of the main objectives of Jezebelites is to gain as many followers as possible, and they will actually court various individuals by posing as their friends or counselors. It is entirely possible to see such a courted individual gradually come under the hypnotic influence of a Jezebelite. Some people are blinded and under the sway of Jezebel, while others become totally immersed and open up to this spirit. Consequently, the principality gains strength, but it is preventable. Ask the Lord to open your eyes, because you can counteract this influence through prayer. Early intervention is the key, so don't disregard the little warning signs.

*Many are familiar with the Holy Spirit, but when confronted with Jezebel, they rely solely on what they see.*

Remember, this can be a gradual process. We Christians can be an unsuspecting lot. We are taught to think the best of the brethren, and we have had it pounded into us that we should not judge one another. That, of course, is true, but it needs to be balanced with the precious gift of discernment. There can be various saints in the congregation who are familiar with the operation of the Holy Spirit, but when confronted with the possibility of a Jezebel in their midst, they rely solely on what they see. Before them stands a longtime friend, a seemingly righteous individual, and a leader who endorses their ministry. Voila! The enemy has just cloaked an entire congregation.

There is also a great deal of kingdom building that comes into play with Jezebel. All of us try to win favor at some point or another, but if you're Spirit-led, He will rein you in. Jezebelites have the ability to draw, sway, and enlist people to their camps. This, by the way, is exactly what begins to happen. They actually have a following of individuals who look to them for spiritual guidance. Those who are more dependent on the Lord do not succumb so easily and do not need the approval of others.

## THOSE OPPOSING JEZEBEL

Soon after the groundwork has been laid, anyone who might stand in the way of the Jezebelite becomes a target. Jezebelites have their own discernment and can tell if you resist their leadership. Many attempts will be made to draw you into the "flock within the flock," but once it is realized that you are independent, there will be a strong sense of rejection. This is a pushing-away process, and many leave as a result.

However, if you are the stalwart type and manage to remain, the second phase of expulsion will begin. The ruling spirit will make continual attempts at discrediting, undermining, and undercutting you as the target. You may be falsely accused, or you may gradually realize that you're being overlooked for various considerations, prophetic words, and so forth. It is also common for the enemy to start dividing and cutting you from others in leadership and from your friends. At first, you may blame yourself for being oversensitive. But after a while, there's a sense that you are a third- or fourth-class citizen within the house of God. It is not your imagination, but rather a result of mind control that operates with this principality. If the Lord placed you in that congregation, however, you should not leave because your feelings are hurt. The Lord made Himself of no reputation, and if you truly are following Him, you will not let this bother you either.

In addition, it is probable that the target will be hindered at every advance in his or her work for the Lord. Some may say that's the enemy's job and he does it to everyone. However, this is not done in general terms, but with the intent of eliminating a threat to this principality. It could be the person's anointing, position, character, or worship. If you have an anointing for worship or even if you are a true worshipper privately, that is cause enough to become a target. The reason for this is that the Lord can use worshippers to dislodge the spirit of Jezebel.

All they need to do is ask the Lord for strength, direction, and wisdom, and He will see them through victoriously to the other side. Unfortunately, many people succumb to the pressure, which can be great, and leave because of ignorance, fear, exhaustion, and other such factors.

If the target happens to be especially resilient, then the troops are called out in the form of extermination, annihilation, eradication, destruction, and dissemination of will. Of course, if you are the target and are unaware of these five weapons, you will probably collapse because your entire focus will be on survival. However, if you ask the Lord for a word of knowledge, a simple binding of these spirits previously mentioned is enough to destroy the enemy's plan.

Another interesting tactic of the enemy via this stronghold is the discrediting, undermining, and destruction of the target's reputation. Just like the Lord can give us favor, so the enemy can attempt to rob us of this and replace it with ill-favor. Unless we are conscious of this possibility, we may not realize what is going on until a bad situation arises. Once this is noticed, it's a fairly simple process of binding this tactic and asking the Lord for more of His favor.

*Give diligent attention to the condition of your family, friends, co-workers, prayer partners, and others.*

It's important to note that as a target of this principality, every area of your life is subject to attack. Do not be naïve and think that it concerns only you and your immediate surroundings. Give diligent attention to the condition of your family, friends, co-workers, prayer partners, and anyone else who offers support. Dismiss any idea that you are being paranoid and overreactive. Loved ones will suffer as a result of this attitude. However, it is possible to detect a pattern, so just begin to cover your family sufficiently. Look for signs of intrusion within your finances, business dealings, favor, relationships, possessions, promotions, and other areas. Jezebel is a principality and seeks to destroy anyone who poses a threat.

At this point, most individuals targeted will probably leave the church *unless* they know what is going on; which, of course, is one of the purposes of this book. Saints need to know the importance of staying in a congregation infected with a Jezebel spirit. Unfortunately, many saints look at the atrocities of war and take off because they are tired, or they consider the injustices and sin as grounds for withdrawal. However, if the Lord has instructed you to stay, do not look at the terrible situation you are in, but rather consider it an honor to be used by the Lord in restoring life to a dead situation. Imagine the Lord's appreciation for withstanding mistreatment in the process of deliverance and restoration of those who were once deceived.

Jezebel in the midst can be overcome and the person used by the enemy can be saved and restored.

# CHAPTER 4—A Company of Elijahs

The prophetic word through Malachi stated that someone special would usher in the coming of the Lord: "Behold, I will send you Elijah the prophet before the coming of the great and dreadful day of the LORD" (Mal. 4:5).

The Scriptures also said that there would be one who would prepare the way of the Lord: "The voice of him that crieth in the wilderness, prepare ye the way of the LORD, make straight in the desert a highway for our God. Every valley shall be exalted, and every mountain and hill shall be made low: and the crooked shall be made straight, and the rough places plain: and the glory of the LORD shall be revealed, and all flesh shall see it together: for the mouth of the LORD hath spoken it" (Isa. 40:3–5). The Lord Himself referred to John the Baptist in the fortieth chapter of Isaiah.

"And his disciples asked him, saying, why then say the scribes that Elias must first come? And Jesus answered and said unto them, Elias truly shall first come, and restore all things. But I say unto you, that Elias is come already, and they knew him not, but have done unto him whatsoever they listed. Likewise shall also the Son of man suffer of them. Then the disciples understood that he spake unto them of John the Baptist" (Matt. 17:10–13).

The Lord explained to the apostles that the spirit of Elijah had come through John the Baptist to introduce His first coming. Richard Ing, author of *Spiritual Warfare* states, along with other men of God, that this shall also be the case at His second coming. As the Holy Spirit operated through Elijah and John the Baptist, so He will operate through a company of Elijahs, or as Ing calls them "sons of God" before the coming of the great and dreadful day of the Lord.

"And the LORD shall utter his voice before his army: for his camp is very great: for he is strong that executeth his word: for the day of the LORD is great and very terrible; and who can abide it?" (Joel 2:11).

Without this knowledge, some would lament that the spirit of Jezebel is attacking the saints because it is so prevalent and can be found in the workforce, in families, and in many churches. If that is your case, then you are looking at this from the wrong perspective. Rejoice! The Lord is coming! Get your eyes off Jezebel and look at what the Lord is doing. He is raising up a company of Elijahs. Many of us have been crying out for revival, not realizing that it was coming through the Elijahs that the Lord is grooming.

What did this great prophet do but turn the idolatrous nation of Israel back to the Lord? In America alone, it is easy to pick out the various forms of idolatry. Whatever takes first place in our hearts and pushes the Lord off to the sidelines is an idol. America needs to return unto the Lord and love Him with all her heart; we are desperately in need of an Elijah company.

Rejoice, America! The Lord is going to deliver us, and He is raising up an army in our very midst. Remember, Elijah prophesied Ahab and Jezebel's demise, and the will of God was unquestionably carried out. At that time, it took only one man used by God to tear down the work of Satan, and now the Lord is using a *company* of Elijahs to prepare the way of the Lord and usher in His second coming.

There is a wonderful book entitled *Elijah: A Man of Heroism and Humility* by Charles R. Swindoll. This book explains how Elijah may have started out with a message from the Lord, but it was through his encounter with Jezebel and Ahab that he was transformed into a man of God. The life that resulted was one of faith and power with God.

*Jezebel is not attacking you, but rather the potter is at work.*

Jezebel is not attacking you, but rather the potter is at work, and He's making you into a vessel that will be able to stand tall in the kingdom of God. Elijah put an end to idol worship in Israel, and the people turned back to the Lord. That's what the spirit of Elijah did through John the Baptist. Now the Lord is preparing a *company* of Elijahs to bring in the second coming of the Lord. Jezebel is around only because the Lord is using that spirit to carve a prophet from a lump of clay.

Elijah bravely challenged Ahab, 450 false prophets, and the nation of Israel on Mount Carmel and then successfully called down fire from heaven. Shortly thereafter, he received a threatening message from Jezebel and took off running. Granted, the spirit of Jezebel carries a strong spirit of fear with it, but this man was brilliant in spiritual battle one minute and cowering the next. The Lord had to work on his character and cause him to remain steadfast in the face of danger. Elijah was a prepared vessel, and Ahab and Jezebel were tools that the Lord used to chisel out His likeness in this beloved prophet. So it is with many of us in this day. The Lord is using modern-day Ahabs and Jezebels to prepare the saints around the world.

However, most importantly, the Elijah company will usher in the second coming of the Lord in holiness. Elijah was a man of the wilderness, as was John the Baptist. They did not hail from the most prestigious rabbinical schools, but rather they were hidden in the wilderness alone with the Father. They heard from Him, and their message was the same: repent. They were known as preachers of holiness. This will be a trademark of the Elijah company prior to the second coming.

"But who may abide the day of his coming? and who shall stand when he appeareth? for he is like a refiner's fire, and like fullers' soap: and he shall sit as a refiner and purifier of silver: and he shall purify the sons of Levi, and purge them as gold and silver, that they may offer unto the LORD an offering in righteousness" (Mal. 3:2–3).

These prophets met the Lord in the wilderness and allowed Him to work in their lives. Anyone embroiled in a spiritual battle with Jezebel will attest to the fact that it is a wilderness experience where you get refined and purified. Outwardly, nothing appears to be happening, and you are cut off from the main flow. It's a place of stripping and of preparation.

If there is junk in your heart or if you are holding out on the Lord, you will find yourself weakening during spiritual conflicts. Stubbornness does not last long because you need the Lord in an encounter with this prince. The Lord will just let you duke it out with this beast for a while. It will not be long before you are asking, "How high, Lord?" Think about what the Lord is preparing us for—His second coming! What is a little pain for such an honor?

If we are being prepared for the Elijah company, then we must have the same traits as Elijah and John the Baptist had. They were not concerned with public opinion or materialism. They were sold out to the Lord. They were brutally honest, holy, and they lived separated lives. As a result, the Lord fulfilled Elijah's prophetic words and withheld rain for three and a half years.

If you are shut up in the wilderness with the Lord because Jezebel has culled you from the congregation and tagged you as a troublemaker, then guess who is going to be your *best* friend and closest buddy? The whole thing is a setup, and Jezebel is instrumental in carrying out the Lord's plan. It gets better. He compensates for your pain by letting you in on His secrets and plans. His presence is especially close, and the turnaround time on your prayers improves. All this is an attempt to offset your separation. It sure sounds like higher ground to me, saints!

Actually, you have been raised to a new and higher level because your circumstances have dictated a closer walk with the Lord. Better yet, you are more in harmony with the Lord and are now able to communicate with Him on a higher level. You are sharper in the Holy Spirit, and you really start hearing from the Lord. (Unfortunately, no one will believe you until the Lord takes you out of the wilderness!)

You will also find that there is a strong desire to see the Lord exalted before the people. This, of course, is in direct opposition to the designs of Jezebel. There is a spirit of seeking supremacy and one-upmanship that comes with this principality. Yet the Elijah company has no desire for recognition because of their close relationship with the Lord. The Lord is enough. They do not need recognition. As a result, they have an ample supply of oil in their lamps—the oil of devotion.

This is also what made Elijah bold. He knew the Lord was his source and not man. He was confident that the Lord would carry out His word.

And so it is today. Those in the Elijah company are sold out to the Lord as a result of an encounter with Jezebel. They are not the same; it is a privilege for them to have the spirit of Elijah worked in their lives by the Lord.

# Chapter 5—Obedience Is Better Than Warfare

As mentioned in the previous chapter, the Lord is raising up a company of Elijahs in the last days, and consequently, there are many people on the potter's wheel. Therefore, we need to concentrate on the Lord rather than on warring all the time. Unfortunately for everyone involved, it can take a while before this becomes evident, as it did for yours truly. We have a tendency to zoom in on other people's faults, overlooking our own. This results in our being totally oblivious to what the Lord is trying to do in our own lives.

"Thou hypocrite, first cast out the beam out of thine own eye; and then shalt thou see clearly to cast out the mote out of thy brother's eye" (Matt. 7:5).

There may be areas in which the Lord is dealing with us, and we have been taking it lightly because we think it is more important to rout Jezebel out of our congregation. In actuality, the Lord may have

39

planted this tool to whittle away on us. Some situations that have cropped up may actually be the Lord's way of trying to get us to turn around.

We might have some serious health issues, financial pressures, family situations, and so forth, and we think that the source is Jezebel. We need to think again. It could be the Lord allowing our enemy to get very close, so we will repent and cry out to the Lord. After all, in the Old Testament, the Lord repeatedly allowed Israel's enemies to encroach on their borders, posing a serious threat to national security, in hopes that they would smarten up and return to Him.

We have been wrestling with Jezebel, but could it be He has been waiting for our obedience? Some of us may have been so stubborn that we have life-threatening circumstances and have even recognized death in the spirit. A great pressure could be an indication of a long resistance or a great need in us.

*There is a direct correlation between the achievement of the Lord's goals and the timing of your deliverance.*

If we would reverse our strategy and cooperate with the Lord, He would release us from the trial much sooner. We need to get it in our heads that He is trying to do a work in us, and the sooner the work is completed, the sooner the situation will be resolved. There is a direct correlation between the achievement of the Lord's goals and our deliverance.

Sometimes, however, all we can see are the terrible injustices, the destruction, and the oppression. We are incensed that this exists in our congregation. There may even be a situation where the Lord is not receiving the glory and honor because a counterfeit spirit exists. Chances are, He is willing to sacrifice this so that we can achieve the development necessary to be part of the Elijah company. He gets great pleasure in a life that He has molded and shaped into His likeness and image. The effects are longer lasting, and His fellowship is eternal.

Unfortunately, too many saints look at the injustices and wrongdoings and walk away. They are pleased with the fact that they have picked up the spirit of Jezebel, and they take off. If they manage to hang around for a while, they wilt once the temperature is turned up. They fail to recognize the trial as a work of the Lord.

It takes determination to allow the Lord to carve out a spirit of Elijah in you. Elijah was known as a man with a rugged spirit, but even if you are a laid-back individual, the Lord can strengthen you to the point that you can face Jezebel. This is possible if you are willing to trust the Lord to make you strong. Elijah's relationship with the Lord and His ability to hear from God got him through.

It is a tremendous privilege for the Lord to develop His character in us, but many times, we balk at the inconvenience. When teaching a child to ride a bike, a father must invest time and patience. The child often fails to recognize the bonding that is taking place. We have to look at our trials and teachings differently. We need to stop our crying because we are going through difficulties and instead cherish the fact that He is very close at that time. He has His eye on us and often takes great pains to work out the necessary details for our lives. Not only that, but He is excited as He sees us change. Earthly fathers get all puffed up as they see their kids mature and take on good qualities. Could that be why He rejoices over us with singing?

> Sing, O daughter of Zion; shout, O Israel; be glad and rejoice with all the heart, O daughter of Jerusalem. The LORD hath taken away thy judgments, he hath cast out thine enemy: the king of Israel, even the LORD, is in the midst of thee: thou shalt not see evil any more. In that day it shall be said to Jerusalem, fear thou not: and to Zion, let not thine hands be slack. The LORD thy God in the midst of thee is mighty; he will save, he will rejoice over thee with joy; he will rest in his love, he will joy over thee with singing.
>
> Zephaniah 3:14–17

Whatever the dealing, we must make sure we follow His instructions. We cannot use our battle against Jezebel as an excuse to ignore the correction of the Lord. The battle will *look like* it must be tended to, but this is a ploy of the enemy. Actually, the reverse is true. We'll get further ahead if we concentrate on obeying the Lord than if we constantly try to beat down the enemy.

Deuteronomy 11:8 says, "Therefore shall ye keep all the commandments which I command you this day, that ye may be strong and go in and possess the land." Verse 25 says, "There shall no man be able to stand before you." All these things are contingent on obedience, and we do not want the opposite of verses 8 and 25 to be true. If we *do not* obey, then we *will not* be strong, and we *will not* go in and possess the land or have victory over Jezebel.

Logic would dictate that we need to pay more attention to the Lord's directives than to the racket of the enemy. Seek ye first the kingdom of God, and all these things shall be added unto you. When you put the Lord's business first, you'll sense that you're out from under oppression. You will still have to do warfare, but balance is the key word.

# CHAPTER 6—Who Shall Stand in His Holy Place?

"Who shall stand in His holy place? He who has clean hands and a pure heart." (Ps. 24:3-4) No matter what injustices are operating within the church, if your heart is holding a grudge, you will not have the ear of the Lord and it will zap you of any spiritual strength. The enemy can do terrible things through the life of a Jezebelite, but *you* must be spotless. Righteousness in itself is a weapon.

His promises are for the righteous, and we cannot expect to beat the enemy if we look and act like him. There will be unbelievably wicked things done by the enemy that will rile our souls to no end, but we will get absolutely nowhere if our hearts are filled with resentment.

> *What good is it if you're some hotshot warrior, but your gates are wide open because of sin?*

During Bible times, there were many walled cities for protection. One of the first tactics of the enemy was to storm the gates to gain entry, and so it is with your enemy. If he can get you to sin, then the gate is open and your protection is compromised. It is of the utmost importance to keep a clean heart before the Lord. What good is it if you are some hotshot prayer warrior, but you are sitting there with your gates wide open because of sin? It is impossible to make progress under those circumstances.

Instead, you need to take inventory on a routine basis to see if any resentment, offense, or sin has slipped past unnoticed. When you are under fire by a spirit of Jezebel, keeping a clean heart is not an option, but a necessity. Actually, it is something you ought to be doing anyway to honor the Lord, because He wants you to live a holy life. Your struggle with this stronghold serves as a training ground because it forces you to form this good habit.

You have to play the game by the Lord's rules if you expect Him to help, and it is impossible to beat this spirit on your own. The Lord has an entirely different standard than the world does. Watch Him. He is tremendously patient and loving and gives people every opportunity before finally exposing them. He does not get mad and respond in retaliation. He does not hold a grudge against us when we do something wrong, but rather He loves us and presents many opportunities for us to turn around.

The Lord by nature is incredibly kind—to the just and the unjust. God sometimes honors us when we do not deserve it. How many times has He been merciful to us even when we never should have received mercy? How many times have we been blessed just because He felt like it and not because we were deserving? The result is that we fall deeper and deeper in love with Him, and His goodness leads us unto repentance.

So why should some of us be shocked or disgruntled when our enemy receives honor or gifts from the Lord while in sin? The reason is, our hearts are not right toward those individuals. Discernment allows us to pick up some terrible things sent our way, and it is difficult to experience this and still maintain a spotless heart toward those individuals. However, God expects us to be perfect, or mature, as He is perfect, and we are to mirror His image as His son or daughter. So get ready for a lot of change. Relinquish your rights and blot out the word *fair* from your vocabulary, because you will not be using it anymore!

Not only is it necessary for an intimate relationship with the Father, but this is crucial because curses, witchcraft, and sorcery are parts of the Jezebel package. We cannot afford to have these things attached to our lives. You might say, "Well, I'll just bind anything sent to me." The problem is that if there is a cause for this curse to be sent, it will stick. But if the vessel is clean, then there is no cause. "As the bird by wandering, and the sparrow by flying, so the curse causeless shall not come" (Prov. 26:2).

If you sense oppression, along with a surreal feeling in your head similar to a spinning sensation, and if everything you do seems to have the opposite of the Midas touch, then there is a good chance you are experiencing the effects of curses, witchcraft, and sorcery. If so, check with the Lord so you can confess your faults and clear up the matter, and then the symptoms will disappear. This is a prime example of how righteousness is a weapon that will protect you and, at the same time, be the undoing of Jezebel.

# CHAPTER 7—The Father's Heart

It is impossible to gain the victory over the spirit of Jezebel without love. In fact, an encounter with this principality will cause you to see the depth of your love. In many cases, people who thought they had a solid love walk will realize it was only a thin veneer.

This wrestling match will bring out the worst in you and enable you to see just how much junk is in your heart. Some of the wounds in this war can be both deep and wide, and you will wonder if you will ever get all the resentment and offense out of your heart. In fact, it will take a total turning away from entertaining any thoughts of resentment in order to overcome a root of bitterness.

The only way to gain ascendancy over this spirit is to operate in instant and consistent forgiveness with every offense. The basis of operation for Jezebel is jealousy and resentment. Therefore, these two sins cannot be found in someone who is trying to rout this principality. However, that prince is going to want you to leave because you are a threat to him. As a result, you will encounter every injustice and offense imaginable. Unless you have purposed in your heart *not* to be offended and are ready to forgive the people the enemy is using, you will definitely fold under the pressure.

Resentment and offense are two of the biggest weapons that the enemy will launch in this war. His arsenal is loaded with this type of missile, and the only way to deflect a blow is to ignore any provocation sent our way. First Corinthians 13:4 says that charity suffereth long. This is why the Lord told us to suffer ourselves to be wronged. Sometimes we think that we are great warriors and are going to pull down strongholds because we have an intercessory spirit; however, in fact, the Lord is using this very situation to work the character of Christ in our lives, and the real weapons of our warfare are love and forgiveness.

*Once you accept the fact that the Lord is allowing all of this, your perspective and reactions change.*

When this entire experience is viewed as a work of the Lord, forgiving and acting in love become easier. It does not mean you will be faultless, but it will put things in proper perspective. It will help you to relax and be more emotionally detached from circumstances. At that point, you'll be more able to cooperate with the Lord. Once you accept the fact that the Lord is allowing and using all of this in your life, your perspective and reactions change.

Your first inclination might be to think that the Lord will deal with the individual housing this Jezebel spirit and those who are supportive of it. However, that is a limited viewpoint. God knows what exists in our hearts, and it is entirely possible that those of us targeted are every bit as controlling and manipulative as the individual with the Jezebel spirit. The Lord can inflict one unjust situation after another to make "control" an intolerable trait. He knows how to eliminate our undesirable characteristics.

You will also notice that the Jezebelite will be treated fairly. The Lord greatly loves those who are held captive by this prince, and we are to have the same attitude.

It is hard to imagine that the Lord would allow a principality to spread, develop, and become so entrenched. Nor would you think that He would allow a congregation to have no significant growth for years. Could there possibly be a greater work of God going on? Yes, and He is in control from start to finish. Despite humiliations, unfair dealings, demotions, cliques, in-fighting, and scratching and clawing, God is at work. He raised up Samuel in less than perfect circumstances, yet he was one of the greatest prophets.

You may think that difficult situations are terrible; however it is often the Lord's way of doing something beautiful in you. Rejection can work compassion in you. It will cause you to reach out to others who are treated unfairly, and it brands your memory so that you act appropriately for years to come.

Sometimes the Lord will sweetly encourage you in order to wean you from some of your bad habits, but many times you are changed through trials. The point is not to be so engrossed with the fact that there is something as ugly as a Jezebel spirit at work. Instead, relax. Look for the Lord, follow Him, and ask for His direction. You will get a lot further ahead. Besides, this is an opportune time to "love your enemies, bless them that curse you . . . use you, and persecute you" (Matt. 5:44).

A congregation can look as though it is all but destroyed by the enemy, yet the Lord can raise it up. Look at the work at Calvary. The enemy thought he had beaten Jesus and destroyed the plan of God when in fact it *was* the plan of God. If it pleased the Lord to bruise His Son and put Him to grief, couldn't He also do this with a congregation? The Lord can carve out a company of Elijahs through the suffering caused by Jezebel.

It is here that you get to know the heart of the Lord. You may have had terrible things launched at you from this spirit, causing you to cry out for the Lord's intervention. Some Jezebelites are so deceived they will not stop until they reach their goal of annihilation. They have hardened their hearts and rationalized their positions. Don't be surprised, however, if you sense He is looking for a man to stand in the gap (Ezek. 22:30).

As painful and destructive as Jezebel can be, the Lord can turn you around to the point that you pray for mercy for those individuals hosting this prince. This is when you know that you are in harmony with the Lord and your heart is beating like His.

He wants you to intercede for those with a Jezebel spirit even though there is a history of atrocities. The Lord has been molding you into His image; therefore, *you* should be crying out for His mercy. This could be termed as having a heart after God's heart because you want what the Lord wants. It is proof to the Lord that there's no resentment left behind and that you are ready to come out of prison.

The Lord's heart is full of compassion. If this Jezebelite was once a child of God, God's heart is breaking. This is one of His children who has gone astray. His love is even greater than the love of an earthly father who laments over a lost or broken relationship. You may be justified in your request of retribution, but look at the opportunity to minister to your heavenly Father. For years He has met your needs; now you can return the favor by crying out for mercy.

In the story of the prodigal son, the father loved the righteous son, despite his resentment. If the eldest son had sought his wayward brother and returned home with him, can you imagine how grateful the father would have been? Simply shift your focus from yourself to your Father. If you intercede for your enemy, don't you think the Lord will protect your family and friends until things are resolved?

# CHAPTER 8—High Praises Put Jezebel in Chains

If you are in the throes of a conflict with a principality such as Jezebel, you will not survive without high praises! Praise is demonstrated as you walk down the hall singing a song unto the Lord, but high praise is a focused attempt to "climb the hill of Zion" and obtain the intimate presence of the Lord. The effects of the latter are tremendous in defeating the enemy that comes against you. Look at what Psalm 149 says:

> Let the high praises of God be in their mouth, and a two-edged sword in their hand;
> To execute vengeance upon the heathen, and punishments upon the people;
> To bind their kings with chains, and their nobles with fetters of iron;

To execute upon them the judgment written: this honour have all his saints. Praise ye the LORD.

Psalm 149:6–9

Those enemy forces that assail us are actually put in chains and fetters. The spirit of Jezebel can be a principality, and these Scriptures refer to kings and nobles, the higher-ranking echelon of Satan's kingdom. Consequently, if the higher ranks of his kingdom are in chains, then so are the vast number of lower-level devils associated with this principality. Verse 9 says that it is an honor for saints to carry out this judgment against the enemy.

Not only do high praises put the enemy in chains for a season, but the high praises of God issue us right into the presence of the Lord. As a result, the enemy is bound, and the mountains, or obstacles, melt like wax at the presence of the Lord. "As smoke is driven away, so drive them away: as wax melteth before the fire, so let the wicked perish at the presence of God" (Ps. 68:2).

Once you have come into the high praises of God and have met with the Lord, you will sense a subsiding of His intimate presence. That means it is time to declare Scripture, promises, and *rhema* words, as well as make your petitions concerning the situation that you are battling. The Scriptures state that it is the high praises of God *and* a two-edged sword that execute judgment against these kings and nobles of the enemy's camp.

It is important to keep a proper perspective when confronted with this principality, and praise does just that. When you praise the Lord, it keeps your eyes and mind on the Lord instead of on your problems. Your mind is filled with His greatness, compassion, mercy, and faithfulness because you are constantly praising Him. As you sing the Lord's praises, you are reciting His attributes, and He becomes bigger than your problems.

Consequently, when that occurs, you are at peace. "Thou wilt keep him in perfect peace, whose mind is stayed on thee: because he trusteth in thee" (Isa. 26:3). Praise causes you to keep your mind on Him, *and* it will also enable you to trust *Him!*

*During a lengthy siege with Jezebel, you're going to need numerous refillings at the praise pumps.*

There is another vital aspect of praise that cannot be overlooked. During a lengthy and strenuous siege with any principality, you are going to need numerous refillings at the praise pumps, because there is nothing like being strengthened and revitalized in the presence of the Lord.

Lastly, praise turns situations around. If the enemy surrounds you, the Lord will deliver when you begin to praise Him. If He did it for Jehoshaphat, then He will do it for you. The people of Ammon, Moab, and Mount Seir rose up against Judah to take the Promised Land, and the Lord had this to say: "Ye shall not need to fight in this battle: set yourselves, stand ye still, and see the salvation of the LORD with you, O Judah and Jerusalem: fear not, nor be dismayed; to morrow go out against them: for the LORD will be with you. And Jehoshaphat bowed his head with his face to the ground: and all Judah and the inhabitants of Jerusalem fell before the LORD, worshipping the LORD" (2 Chron. 20:17–18).

The chapter continues in verse 22: "And when they began to sing and to praise, the LORD set ambushments against the children of Ammon, Moab, and mount Seir, which were come against Judah; and they were smitten."

It is common to feel surrounded by the enemy and completely closed in, but if you praise the Lord, you will begin to win. It is not a lighthearted little ditty that needs to be sung, but rather it is a true song of praise. It takes full concentration, wholeheartedness, and determination, and you should not stop until you break through. It is done often with much exuberance and force involving the entire body. Watch your physical gestures because they are often indicative of what is taking place in the spirit and are quite necessary.

There is a real battle that ensues, and the enemy will try to make you feel that you are not making any headway; but just bind anything that might try to block your praise and cut you off from the Lord. If you persist, the Lord will come on the scene, because the Word says He inhabits the praises of His people. Sometimes, however, He may hesitate a little in order to build your endurance and increase your strength. *Then* He comes in with His sweet and intimate presence.

Sometimes the Holy Spirit will drop a beautiful song of deliverance in your heart. It is a real blessing for Him to do this because then you can sing this song all day as you do your work and find yourself mounting up with wings of eagles. The Lord often delivers with such a song of praise, so don't let it slip away. It brings great delight!

There are times, however, when the warfare gets particularly rough. It is not a pleasant experience, and carrying on everyday functions becomes difficult, if not almost impossible. Fortunately, this does not happen all the time, but it often occurs when those opposing you are making an all-out effort to gain territory in the spirit realm. Though you could respond with intense and sustained warfare, consider taking this golden opportunity to offer a costly sacrifice of praise before the Lord.

He knows what has transpired, and He knows your anxiety and frustration. He also knows that you are one step away from bitterly complaining about the unfairness of your situation. However, consider this alternative to such a negative response: when you lay it all aside and enter into His gates with thanksgiving and His courts with praise, you cause a particularly sweet fragrance to waft before His throne.

It is like receiving an intricate handmade gift that took a great deal of time to fashion. It's the love, time, and effort expended that make the gift valuable. The same is true of a sacrifice of praise during difficult times of warfare. Most of us, however, would rather blame the Lord when we are overwhelmed with intense oppression.

David said that he would not make an offering before the Lord unless it cost him something. Undoubtedly, this type of praise will cost you. "And the king said unto Araunah, Nay; but I will surely buy it of thee at a price: neither will I offer burnt offerings unto the LORD my God of that which doth cost me nothing. So David bought the threshing floor and the oxen for fifty shekels of silver" (2 Sam. 24:24).

King David was not religious, nor was he going through the motions of making an offering. He considered the value of his gift, and we need to do so as well. When the gift is costly because of increased warfare, the song becomes more beautiful before the Lord. What joy it must bring Him when we place our pain to the side and enter into His praise! It means He is more precious than our problem and that we trust Him. It is costly, but most pleasing to Him. Consequently for us, praising Him out of a sincere heart of love is probably the fastest way to get this demonic oppression to lift.

# CHAPTER 9—Declare Unto the Heavenlies

There will be no stopping you if you regularly declare in the heavenlies what God has spoken to you. It is the creative word of God and, therefore, heavy artillery in the spiritual realm. If the Lord has spoken to you in your spirit or through a *rhema* word, a prophetic word, or a dream, then He *will* bring it to pass.

Consequently, the Lord wants you to declare His word. He says, "Call those things that are not as though they were" (Rom. 4:17). When the Lord gives a prophetic word or a *rhema* word, He expects you to pray for its fulfillment *and* to declare it into the atmosphere. This applies to a word spoken for the body of Christ or to an individual.

There is creative ability in the spoken Word of God as we see in the first three verses of Genesis. This is something He does, and He expects us to follow suit. "And God said, Let there be light: and there was light" (Gen. 1:3).

The creative word is important. If the Lord has spoken a word of promise to you and there is no material evidence of such a thing, then you need to declare the spoken word into the atmosphere because it has creative abilities. When you proclaim what God has spoken, it is an act of faith to declare it in the spiritual realm. You are proclaiming loud and clear to both the Lord and the host of darkness.

The Lord spoke to the things that were not as though they were. All through the Gospels, Jesus spoke and people were healed. It was His spoken Word. He had the necessary faith, and things happened. Where there had been destruction, suddenly life and health were evident.

Second, when spoken, the Word of God is sharper than a two-edged sword, and it cuts in the spirit realm. It is a form of warfare and very similar to brandishing a sword in the air. The enemy melts right before your eyes. He simply cannot stand up to the Word.

"In the beginning was the Word, and the Word was with God, and the Word was God" (John 1:1). This passage is talking about Jesus. Some situations may take longer than others or may need the prayer of agreement, but the principle always works. God's Word does not come back to Him void but always produces that which He desires.

So, if it appears that the plans of the Lord have been compromised in any way, then we are expected to declare the creative Word of the Lord. Ezekiel demonstrated this in the story of the dry bones. He prophesied to a dry, lifeless situation, and what he said came to pass. We can expect to see the same identical miracle in our circumstances!

"So I prophesied as he commanded me, and the breath came into them, and they lived, and stood up upon their feet, an exceeding great army" (Ezek. 37:10).

If you are standing in faith for a promise and there seems to be a holdup, then you need to inquire of the Lord. It may be that He is doing a deeper work in your life, which takes longer, or it could be that another individual is declaring the same thing erroneously. Ask for wisdom and give everyone the benefit of the doubt. If the Lord has spoken a word to you, then He will keep His promise.

"The LORD of hosts hath sworn, saying, Surely as I have thought, so shall it come to pass; and as I have purposed, so shall it stand" (Isa. 14:24).

"For the LORD of hosts hath purposed, and who shall disannul it? and his hand is stretched out, and who shall turn it back?" (Isa. 14:27).

Sometimes an innocent individual will start naming and claiming without checking with the Lord, or it could be people with a Jezebel spirit who are operating out of the soul realm with their declarations. All this has to be determined and then handled appropriately. Rest assured, their declarations will have an effect in the spirit because of the following Scripture: "Death and life are in the power of the tongue" (Prov. 18:21).

But whatever the case, if the Lord has spoken to you, declare His word, for it is powerful and will bring to pass the will of God for your life. Here are just a few pointers when declaring God's word. Make sure that all blocks, bondages and incapacitations, in general, are bound from you. Specifically bind anything that would stand before you to block your declarations of faith. Sometimes the enemy will send the spirit of doubt and unbelief to block your declarations. Merely bind these things and be on your way. It is also important to disannul anyone's claim to the promise the Lord has made to you. In addition, it is actually possible for Jezebelites to steal your promise through their prayers and declarations. You need to check in the spirit to see if any of these things have occurred.

As you declare the promises of God, there should be an excitement in your heart to encourage you. If it's not there, then one of the above things has happened. Another possibility is that you're sensing the opposition from the Jezebelite who is praying or declaring at the same time.

Erroneous declarations by others may slow you down and could potentially alter things if left unchecked, but if you continue to believe and quote the word of God spoken to you, victory will come your way. "Who saith and it cometh to pass if God commandeth it not?" (Lam. 3:37).

If an individual hosting a Jezebel spirit is naming and claiming that which the Lord has spoken to your heart, then it is your responsibility to stand your ground, either corporately or individually. If these false claims are unchallenged, the enemy will produce false evidence, and if you believe what you see with your eyes, then you will lose your promise!

Often Jezebelites are conscious of your opposition because they pick it up in the spirit realm. If they persist, they have closed their conscience. At that point, they become responsible for their actions, and their hearts can become callous and cold. They might make an attempt to maintain a godly walk, but as time goes by, the falsehood becomes apparent to many. Eventually, if you continue to stand, Jezebel's only option is to obliterate you from the scene. This is where the scriptural parallel in 2 Chronicles 13 becomes evident.

Second Chronicles 13 demonstrates the right of believers to stand and believe the Lord for that which was spoken, despite the fact that another believer is opposing them. In II Chronicles 13, King Jeroboam of Israel threatened King Abijah of Judah. It was said that Jeroboam at one time had the favor of God and man, but he was greedy and began to deal treacherously with people.

Before the battle, Abijah began declaring to Jeroboam's army that they could not prosper in their attempt to take the throne away from a descendant of David because of God's promise. He also pointed out that they were worshippers of a golden calf. This calf, of course, came about because of Jeroboam's greed. He wanted what he wanted, and nothing was going to stand in the way. He had been deceptive in his dealings concerning his attempt to obtain the throne.

He was unrighteous and worshipped a golden calf, which means he loved something above the Lord.

*Even if you're outnumbered, declare the promise of God, walk righteously, and the Lord will deliver you.*

While Abijah made his declarations and took a stand against his foe, Jeroboam's army sandwiched him in. The army of Judah cried unto the Lord, blew their trumpets, and the Lord routed Jeroboam all the way to Bethel and Ephron, despite the fact that they had twice as many men as did Judah. Jeroboam never again regained his strength during his reign. So, even if you are outnumbered, declare the promise of God, walk righteously, and the Lord *will* deliver you.

In summary, there is something exciting about trumpeting the Word of the Lord and heralding the truth. It is creative in a positive way and is the beginning of the substance of those things hoped for, and at the same time, it puts the work of the enemy to flight. When the enemy has gotten you down, you can kick into another gear by shouting, praising, speaking in tongues, and declaring the Word of God. Suddenly the atmosphere will clear, and you will be in the joy of the Lord. Meanwhile, the angels of the Lord are taking off to carry out the Word of the Lord. A completely new arena is taking place in the spiritual realm. If however, you receive a word from the Lord and just sit on it, the reverse will happen in the enemy's camp.

He expects us to get involved with His Word by praying and declaring what He has spoken. That way we can share the joy of witnessing something develop out of nothing. It is His way of doing things. He spoke the Word and things were created, and His Word in our mouths does the same thing. Jesus spoke the Word, and people were healed and delivered. He told us that we would do even greater things. Why? Because the Lord dwells within us, and when we declare His Word, things will happen. We should not be shocked. We are His sons and daughters, so why shouldn't we do some of the same things? Speak the Word of God, and bring things to pass that do not yet exist. It is thrilling and truly the abundant life of Jesus!

# CHAPTER 10—Who Is in Control of Your Emotions?

One of the biggest favors you can do for yourself as a Christian is to learn how to control your emotions. Life in general will be much easier, and you won't end up in a ditch quite so often.

When in the world, we often heard such phrases as "If it feels good, do it" or "Let your emotions go. Don't hold back." As Americans, we do little in the way of restraining ourselves. Do not get me wrong. There certainly are times in life that call for a release of emotion as part of the healing process. But generally, there is a need for more balance in the area of emotional control. It is possible that we are not even aware that we have runaway emotions. Today people brag about how wild they can get, and various heritages pride themselves for their emotional displays.

We are so used to demanding our rights that people tell others off several times a day. We live in a world where road rage is a common term. We have television shows that depend on the hostile behavior of their guests in order to maintain their ratings. It is quite common to hear defense lawyers plead temporary insanity for their clients. They are probably right, because if you consistently give your emotions free rein, you get closer and closer to the edge. We even joke about the fact that "we lost it."

*The feeling realm is the enemy's area of expertise and the launching pad for his attacks against mankind.*

What people do not realize is that they are playing right into the enemy's hand. The feeling realm is his area of expertise and the launching pad for his attacks against mankind. When the forces of hell want to destroy, hinder, or impede, they target the mind and the emotions of a person. Therefore, as Christians we need to be very mindful of this and learn to discipline ourselves. But for someone who is facing the spirit of Jezebel, it is not merely recommended—it is an absolute necessity!

The very nature of the spirit of Jezebel is controlling. It sets out to control others for its own purposes, but it will also attempt to control those that pose a threat. If you are a target because you are trying to pull down this prince, the enemy will try to discredit and undermine your work and reputation. This will hurt, but you will certainly lose all credibility if you crumble emotionally. If you take offense and begin worrying, you are in trouble. Offense will cost you spiritual strength, and worry will wear you out. Emotional control is something that you can acquire gradually, but the sooner the better, because along with discrediting and undermining comes the spirit of accusation. These things can come out of nowhere, and suddenly you find yourself embroiled in a destructive situation that calls for a steady head and a clear line of communication with the Lord.

Remember, the purpose of the enemy is to destroy, exterminate, and annihilate, if at all possible. It is like wrestling with an alligator or bear. It is not going to let you catch your breath, and there will be only one survivor. So, you *must* have control of yourself and your emotions.

However, there are levels in this wrestling match, and you eventually mature in the Lord and gain strength. In the beginning, that which opposes you looks like a monster, but as time goes on, you gain strength almost imperceptibly. Then one day you realize that things don't bother you as before.

Case in point: Fear is a big component of the enemy's offensive. It is one of the dominant spirits, along with a few dozen minor spirits that accompany it. If you are not a seasoned veteran in spiritual warfare and this thing hits you, it can actually cause you to break out in a cold sweat with tremors in your arms and legs. The intensity can be so great that you might think you're on the verge of losing your mind.

It is one thing to bind fear and purpose in your heart not to yield to it, but when that adrenaline is pumping and you are trembling, it's an entirely different story. However, there are 365 "fear nots" in the Bible, and they are all commands. We have to truly believe that when we bind something in Jesus' name, it is bound. In conjunction with this, the feeling realm is Satan's domain. If you have bound fear and you still *feel* afraid, then what you are feeling is a lie; so just shut down your emotions in the name of the Lord.

Along the same lines, when you are scoping things out in the spirit, you are open; so if you feel an attack coming, close down and this will turn off your feelers, or antennae, in the spirit realm. Some people do just the opposite when they feel an attack coming and keep their sensors wide open, which only serves to magnify any sensations. After a while, you will gain experience, until one day you realize that the mouse and the monster roles have been reversed. In the beginning, fear appears the size of a monster, and you are the mouse. After a while, there is a greater understanding that you are more than a conqueror. It comes as the Lord strengthens you and you gain experience. However, gaining control of yourself and reining in your emotions help immensely.

When dealing with a Jezebel spirit, you will face many circumstances that will require self-control. One of these areas involves speaking before the congregation. Rest assured, there will be an attempt to control you in the hopes of diminishing your effectiveness. People will attempt to throw things at you in the spirit or bind you as you speak. You will have to be as rugged in spirit as Elijah and know who you are in the kingdom of God.

You will find in dealing with this Jezebel spirit that there are those who do not want you to succeed in your work for the Lord. In fact, they want to overthrow you so they or one of their puppets can take your spot. The bottom line is, they want you out. We have all been up against people who we know are not rooting for us or even those who are in competition with us. We merely stand our ground and maintain our confidence. However, it is an entirely different scenario when you are being confronted by a Jezebelite. We are talking about a principality trying to unseat you. This is an unseen force at work, and you may be the only one experiencing its pressure. It can be a wild ride if you are not ready for it.

When you attempt to speak before a group or make a presentation of any kind, a mature Jezebelite can wage a staggering offense. You will have trouble formulating a clear sentence. Your mind may go blank, and nothing comes together or falls into place. What you may not know is that you are being bound and gagged in the spirit by Jezebel.

Under normal circumstances, a speaker can gradually establish a flow in the presentation as the audience responds with interest. However, when a Jezebel spirit is in operation, the opposite exists. Not only is the speaker bound and incapacitated in the spirit, but those who are under Jezebel's spiritual influence will be disinterested as well. This is witchcraft and sorcery at work right in the middle of a sermon. Those in the audience who are under the sway of Jezebel will never know that they are being controlled. If there are other targets of Jezebel who have experienced this firsthand, they will probably recognize why the speaker is having a hard time and hopefully pray.

Dutch Sheets describes this very thing in *Watchman Prayer*. He states that he encountered a similar experience with witchcraft and sorcery, but fortunately, he had some intercessors with him who were warring for him while he spoke. But what if you are by yourself, or what if you're the only one in the congregation who has discerned this principality and no one else believes you? They would surely call you "loony tunes" if you described what you were experiencing in the spirit. That is when the fun begins!

It will take all that you have to restrain yourself and maintain your composure when a Jezebelite unleashes sorcery and witchcraft prayers against you while you are trying to bring forth a message. However, if you are totally convinced that you have authority over the enemy, then you can learn to stand in the face of this intimidating situation. Unfortunately, in the early stages, many people are unaware that they have encountered a Jezebel spirit and are overwhelmed by the magnitude of the opposition. As a result, it takes them some time before they size up the situation and then additional time and effort before they are able to take a proper stand. Knowing who you are in Christ will enable you to take the proper position that the Lord has obtained for you. This can be acquired only by studying the Word of God.

# CHAPTER 11—Take Every Thought Captive

We have heard countless times that the outcome of the battle has a lot to do with our thought life. And most of us would agree, but keeping a neat and tidy loft is a full-time job. Between the junk we put into our minds and the numerous suggestions the enemy comes up with, it takes all our effort to rid ourselves of "stinkin' thinkin'."

Yet vain imaginations are common among saints. These are thoughts that are completely bogus and have no validity; they are thoughts that run rampant because of fear—false evidence appearing real, as Joyce Meyer would say. Generally, they are seeds planted by the enemy (or our stupidity) to get us out of faith and into emotional reasoning.

The Word of God says that we should bring every thought into captivity: "Casting down imaginations, and every high thing that exalteth itself against the knowledge of God, and bringing into captivity every thought to the obedience of Christ" (2 Cor. 10:5).

It is wholly possible to become so wrapped up in your problems that your mind runs away with itself. This, of course, is exactly what the enemy wants because Isaiah 26:3 says, "Thou wilt keep him in perfect peace, whose mind is stayed on thee." The enemy will try to surround you with circumstances appearing very real and then plague you with fear, doubt, and unbelief. This is a frequently used tool in the Jezebel camp, and soon your mind is running rampant. If you do not learn to rein in your thoughts, it won't be long before defeat will be cheering you on. It is important to recognize this pattern, bind the obvious spirits in operation, and do warfare by refusing the vain imaginations.

If you do not like that suggestion, think of the alternative. You can sit there and wade in the muck and the mire that you and the enemy have created. Of course, this leads to depression, and before you know it, you are the one who is bound instead of the other way around. You sat around all day, eating, watching television, and leading an otherwise totally unproductive day. By this time, your spiritual strength has been drained because you have sowed to the flesh, and now you couldn't fight your way out of a paper bag! Does this sound familiar? It is the enemy's way of keeping you earthbound when you should be seated in heavenly places in Christ Jesus.

If this is the case, just take the Lord at His Word. If He says He has forgiven you, then He has. Put things behind you, and start praising the Lord—and the sooner the better.

The following is an excerpt from the book of Exodus, chapter 34 and verses 12–15, that clearly describes how we can be led astray in our thinking and how offensive a matter this can be to our heavenly Father. Keep in mind that vain imaginations exalt themselves against the knowledge of God. If we believe what the vain imaginations say, then we are not believing the Lord. These thoughts, if exalted above the Lord, are gods.

> Take heed to thyself, lest thou make a covenant with the inhabitants of the land whither thou goest, lest it be for a snare in the midst of thee: but ye shall destroy their altars, break their images, and cut down their groves: for thou shalt worship no other god: for the LORD, whose name is Jealous, is a jealous God: lest thou make a covenant with the inhabitants of the land, and they go a whoring after their gods and do sacrifice unto their gods, and one call thee, and thou eat of his sacrifice. Ex 34:15

It really is a visitor ("one call thee") that comes to you and makes a suggestion that is contrary to what the Lord has spoken. Of course, it brings a few friends such as discouragement, doubt, and others. These inhabitants of the land invite you to think upon a lie, and if you persist in this vein, then you actually go where they want you to go. Where do they want you to go? Well, to pay homage to their god, of course. How do you do that? By believing what their god has said about the matter.

*If you allow vain imaginations to stay, then you're honoring the father of lies.*

If you believe their lie, then you honor the father of lies. The Lord likens this to a form of adultery ("go a whoring") because you are denying the word of the Father and honoring another god. In Old Testament days, making a sacrifice was a form of worship. If you honor the father of lies by deliberately allowing vain imaginations to lodge in your thought life, then you are honoring him, and that is the equivalent of sacrificing to another god.

You are right. This is a lot more serious than originally thought and should be avoided at all costs. It is detrimental to you and to your relationship with the Lord. The enemy will dismiss it as minor and lead you to believe that everybody has a pity party occasionally, but think how hurtful it is to the Lord of the universe when you don't believe what He says to you. In essence, you are calling God a liar. Listen to what the Lord has to say about the matter: "This evil people, which refuse to hear my words, which walk in the imagination of their heart, and walk after other gods, to serve them, and to worship them . . ." (Jer. 13:10).

Much of spiritual warfare involves self-control. In this case, we can win the battle if we control our thoughts. Monitor the contents of your mind from time to time, and be deliberate about your meditations. Do not tolerate anything that is not pure, honest, or of good report. Give no ground to the enemy.

"Finally, brethren, whatsoever things are true, whatsoever things are honest, whatsoever things are just, whatsoever things are pure, whatsoever things are lovely, whatsoever things are of good report; if there be any virtue, and if there be any praise, think on these things " (Phil. 4:8). The Lord put this verse is His Bible for a reason.

# CHAPTER 12—Suffer Yourself to Be Wronged

If the Lord has allowed a Jezebel spirit to exist in your congregation or in any other area of your life, then you are going to suffer until you are delivered. When you allow the Lord to do a deeper work in your life, it takes time, and this is a form of waiting on the Lord. Most people will run rather than put up with pain and heartache. However, if you stay and allow the Lord to do a work in you, then you are waiting on the Lord.

Isaiah 40:31 says that those who wait upon the Lord will renew their strength. We *exchange* our strength for His. Trials are good for us because we come to the startling realization that we cannot get through the ordeal without Him. This is when He has to exchange our strength for His strength.

This is exactly how the Lord fulfills 1 Peter 5:6–10, which says that we are to humble ourselves under the mighty hand of God and resist the enemy who seeks to devour us. The result is that the God of all grace will perfect, establish, strengthen and settle us. Trials are the means He uses to accomplish this. He exchanges our strength for His strength when we cry out for help and allow ourselves to be worked upon.

Not only do we acquire strength when we are in a trial or in the furnace of affliction, but there is also a refining process that takes place. Because of the host of spirits that accompany Jezebel, it is possible to take a beating, depending on where you are in the Lord. With deception come sorcery, witchcraft, false prophecy, and false accusations, and if you are one of the targets, then it is going to be painful.

However, in 1 Peter 2:19–23, the Lord says there will be times when you will suffer wrongly, but if you bear it patiently, then the Father will be pleased. Jesus Himself left us an example that we should follow in His footsteps. He did nothing wrong, and He did not retaliate when treated unfairly; instead, He trusted His Father. Our goal should be to please the Father and allow ourselves to be molded into His image.

This is foreign to the American way of life. Many encounter this principality and walk away because they do not accept hard times and difficulties. In America, we live for pleasure, and some of the more popular topics preached today involve blessing and prosperity. Nevertheless, the Scriptures say that He knows the way that we take, and when He has tried us, we shall come forth as gold (Job 23:10). When gold is tried, it is made pure and increases in value. Yet we struggle with this concept. First Peter 1:7 says that the trial of our faith is more precious than gold. It only gets genuine or pure through trials. A wrestling match with the principality of Jezebel will definitely make the dross come to the surface, but in the end you will be a beautiful gold vessel before the Lord.

This is another way of saying that we are being made perfect, or mature. That is why we look at the character of some polished men and women of God and wonder how they got there. This is how! They did not run when trials came, but they allowed the Lord to do a work.

As saints in the kingdom of God, we need to have a different view of suffering. It brings about a softness and a fragrance in our lives that cannot be obtained any other way. Those saints who have allowed the Lord to work in their lives have a sweetness about them. They have been broken, and there is no haughtiness. They are meek and lowly of heart.

The Lord desires that we be like Him. Listen to Matthew 11:29: "Take my yoke upon you and learn of me; for I am meek and lowly in heart: and ye shall find rest unto your souls." These are the very qualities individuals exhibit when they allow themselves to go through trials and sufferings.

*Without a crushing, there's no sweet and intoxicating aroma.*

Without a crushing, there is no sweet and intoxicating aroma. The trial of our faith only lasts for a season, and the rewards far outweigh the pain. Some people will not let Him work on them because they want only His prosperity and blessings, so that is as far as He can go with them. He blesses them, but they remain in a lower place. However, the ones who allow the Lord to work in their lives get the higher place *and* a double portion of blessing and prosperity. Isn't that what happened to Job? The Lord allowed Satan to have a field day in his life, but in the end, he received double blessings.

It is viewed as a crushing because your brothers and sisters are under the influence of Jezebel and are deceived. As a result, you will appear as the enemy in their eyes. What if the Lord asks you to stand against Jezebel so the enemy doesn't overrun the church? Will you take the rejection or run because it is uncomfortable?

Take it a step further. Will you continue to love them and act as normal as possible, or will you make the mistake of withdrawing to avoid being wounded? If you withdraw, then you could cause further division in the body of Christ. No matter how painful, it's important to remain open and approachable and take your proper position in the body. The Word of God says to love your enemies.

It is one of the hardest things to put yourself in harm's way. You do not have to be a punching bag for someone, but neither can you withdraw yourself from members of the congregation. It is up to you to stay in tune with the Holy Spirit and respond positively when the situation calls for it. This is difficult because you will witness much posturing, false prophecy, and wrong attitudes in an attempt to acquire some status. If nothing else, you have to stand and act in a godly manner to demonstrate the contrast, thus pointing out the falsehood of the other party.

In addition to that, there will be a definite attempt to discredit you and run you out of town, but it all comes down to forgiveness and keeping a clean heart before the Lord. This is what He meant by overcoming evil with good. These individuals often have a mixture, and your good behavior serves as conviction without your uttering a word. People will not listen to you if they know you are angry with them, but they will listen if they know you love them.

This particular course in the school of the Holy Spirit will either kill you or cure you. It is guaranteed to purge you of any resentment because that is the only way you are going to get the victory. When you suffer or allow yourself to be wronged but then forgive, it destroys the ammunition of the enemy.

Be encouraged. When you lose the love and respect of your brothers and sisters and they exclude you from their fellowship because you are willing to stand for the sake of righteousness, Scripture says that your reward in heaven is great! Consequently, if you leave without the Lord's direction, then you are satisfying your flesh and your feelings. Scripture says those who try to save their lives will lose them, and those who lose their lives shall save them. There is a great deal of weeding out and discerning of motives when the Lord allows a Jezebel in your life for a season. You may think the enemy has hit your church, but it is really the Lord sifting out the impurities and showing you what is in your heart.

Regrettably, there will be those saints who will leave when they encounter the mess surrounding this principality. However, they need to discuss their findings with the pastor before taking off. Unfortunately, this is not what happens. Generally, Christians do not want to cause trouble or speak ill about someone else, so they just leave the church. They do not want the pastor to think badly of them, so they give a secondary reason. What an injustice to the man or woman of God if you remain silent about a network of spirits looming over the church! The correct thing is to stand against this principality, but if you are unable to do so, at least discreetly tell the pastor what you have discerned, because it is very possible that Jezebel has duped him or her.

When we are new Christians, we can expect a great deal of pampering, but as older saints, we do not have the right to leave because things get tough. If the Lord put you in a particular congregation, then you are expected to stay until He releases you. If you leave before His timing, then you are in rebellion. This holds true even if there is a lot of ungodly behavior going on. We are not guaranteed a utopian state just because we are in the house of the Lord.

The Lord looked to our redemption as He hung on the cross, so we need to look at the result of our trial as well. We are talking about wrestling in the spirit realm with the principality of Jezebel, just as Elijah did. He was one of the greatest men of God in the Old Testament. Get your mind off the problems and look to the rewards, like he did.

If the Lord changed him and brought him through, He will do the same for you, if you will trust Him. Remember, he won, and so will you! Not only that, but Elijah had one of the best relationships with the Lord because of the dealings he went through. He was also one of the few people in Scripture who did not see death, because his walk brought pleasure to the Lord. It is a privilege to trust the Lord and to walk this path.

This whole matter of enduring suffering will surely separate the men from the boys. It will demonstrate to the Lord whether you are serious about walking with Him. It is wonderful to feel His beautiful presence, take in His blessing, and be filled with His joy. However, if you do not embrace the trials and allow Him to work out the imperfections, then you are merely a fair-weather friend, and your growth will be stunted.

# CHAPTER 13—Love the Lord With All Your Heart

It is entirely possible to love the Lord, yet get yourself so entangled in the grips of warfare that He gradually gets pushed to the back. It may be the furthest thought from your mind, but it can happen. If it does, this can be one of the biggest obstacles to eliminating this principality from your midst because now the battle has become an idol—the very sin of Jezebel herself. You cannot get the victory without the Lord, so be careful not to leave Him somewhere behind.

"I know thy works, and thy labour, and thy patience, and how thou canst not bear them which are evil: and thou hast tried them which say they are apostles, and are not, and hast found them liars: and hast borne, and hast patience, and for my name's sake hast laboured, and hast not fainted. Nevertheless I have somewhat against thee, because thou hast left thy first love" (Rev. 2:1–5).

Unless you have had experience dealing with this principality, you might not even be aware that this could possibly happen. After all, most of us try to guard ourselves against this type of thing. Nevertheless, when you are getting attacked on all sides and so are your friends, family, and prayer partners, it is imperative that you pray and intercede. The warfare can become very intense with serious health issues, financial matters, demotions, false accusations, and even the threat of death.

*He doesn't train us to pull down strongholds just so we'll be totally self-sufficient.*

The Lord wants us to *trust* Him. He does not train us to pull down strongholds so that we will be totally self-sufficient and just drop in to say hello occasionally when the battle subsides. We have to remember that He is God of the universe and has all power to help us. We are His children, and He loves us. Earthly fathers generally love to help their kids, and so it is with the Lord. It is His desire to help us.

Therefore, it is even more important to keep up our love relationship with the Lord than it is to pray and intercede. We will get further if we just seek the Lord for His beauty and wallow in His presence, oblivious to our problems. This kind of attitude is the ultimate of trust. We can say we trust the Lord, but if we are praying and declaring just to relieve the pressure and obtain our goal, then our love statements start to sound tinny.

A similar situation can be found in Haggai when the Lord reproved the people for not building His temple after they had returned to Israel. The Lord told them they had been so busy building their own houses that His lay in waste (Hag. 1:3–4).

The Lord speaks of two things here. The first one refers to your praying and warring for solutions and therefore neglecting to build the Lord a house of praise and worship. You are tending to your house first instead of to His. Cultivate the presence of the Lord. Practice walking in the presence of the Lord. Rid yourself of doubt and worry. Stop trying to work it out by doing this or that; instead, declare the Word of God for your situation and worship the Lord. Trust the Lord in your situation. It is the ultimate step of faith. Go after Him for the sake of spending time just with Him and having no petitions in mind. This is what is meant by building the house of the Lord!

The Lord goes on to say in Haggai 1:8–11 that the people had sown much but brought in little, only to put it into a bag with holes. In other words, they were doing all this work for themselves, but the Lord created a lack because the building of His temple had been virtually ignored. As a result, they were spinning their wheels. When their mistake was recognized and confessed, then He told them to go up the mountain and bring wood that His house might be built and He be glorified. The same can be true of us when we are consumed with warfare. We might find ourselves getting nowhere fast because the Lord has put "holes in our bags."

When Zerubabbel and Joshua, the high priest, heard the word of the Lord, they feared the Lord and immediately began working on His house (Hag. 1:9–12). Shortly thereafter in verse 13, the Lord said that He was with them. If you are wrestling with the enemy, it is important that the Lord be with you. The implication is that the Lord is not fighting for you when you are more concerned with warfare and your own problems than with the Lord, which, of course, puts you on dangerous ground.

Another aspect of building the house of the Lord concerns not only our adoration of the Lord, but the actual work of the Lord. Some have become so bogged down with problems that the work that the Lord has told them to do has been impeded. We need to put this problem aside, trust and praise the Lord, *and do what the Lord has told us to do.* We must build the corporate house of the Lord, as well as our individual temples of praise and prayer.

It is interesting to note that the word of the Lord mentioned in Haggai 1:2–3 was spoken on the first day of the *sixth* month. It says that the Lord stirred up Zerubbabel and Joshua to do the work of the Lord, and it was dated the *twenty-fourth day of the sixth month* in the same year (Hag. 1:15). The people continued to work, and by the *twenty-fourth day of the ninth month,* they had laid the foundation for the house of the Lord. Then the Lord spoke again and told the people in Haggai 2:19, "From this day [forth] will I bless you."

He blessed them on the day they completed the foundation. He did not wait until the entire structure was completed. He wanted to encourage His people to continue in the right direction (Hag. 2:18–19). The Lord can restore you to your rightful position quickly as a result of consistent obedience.

# CHAPTER 14—Business as Usual

With this principality, it is necessary to guard yourself against subtle influences, one of which is an attempt to hinder your work for the Lord. Whether your work is small or great, suddenly it becomes burdensome and difficult to carry out. There seems to be a lack of clarity on how to proceed, and it's as if your head is stuck in a cloud limiting your vision. You forget to do some of the necessities, and a general lethargy and disinterest surrounds you. Overall, it feels as if you are bucking eighty-miles-per-hour headwinds. You do not feel like working on the project at all, and a real sense of dislike and disinterest starts to settle in. Next you begin to feel guilty, and soon there is a distancing in your relationship with the Lord. Sound familiar? Did you think you were just being lazy?

In actuality, what you have experienced is the operation of witchcraft and sorcery. This upsets some people, but it is merely characteristic of this principality. Bind it and go about your business. As this principality begins to weaken, these effects weaken also.

We cannot use the enemy's activity as an excuse, nor should we allow ourselves to come under its influence. This nondescript sense of lethargy can come over you almost daily. You feel like you cannot get much done, but the whole thing is a lie.

Push right past this, because in essence there is little or no resistance. It is nothing but a hoax. It is like bullies who intimidate talented kids because they recognize the kids' potential. If the kids are smart, they will not allow the bullies to box them in, but with a little effort, they will find a way to get around the situation and give their opponents no mind.

Most importantly, don't let your feelings dictate to you, and don't become preoccupied with what you are sensing in the spirit. Instead, press forward regardless. It is necessary to be cognizant of what is going on behind the scenes, but focus on Him and what He wants you to accomplish.

The Scriptures show us that the Lord was strongly opposed by the religious leaders of His day, and they were undoubtedly praying against Him with all kinds of evil sent His way in the spirit realm. All of hell was focused on Him. They criticized the good He did, undermined His ministry, and even said He was of the devil's camp. Individuals posed seemingly innocent questions in the hope of discrediting Him before the multitudes. Yet the spirit of discernment allowed Him to pick up their evil intentions, and

He adroitly turned the tables on them with a simple answer. The Lord is famous for taking the wise in their own craftiness (Job 5:13).

*Jesus never let the enemy hold Him back from doing the Father's work, and neither should we.*

He never said anything except what the Father spoke to Him, so we can use His life as an example and expect the Father to give us wisdom to handle our situations. As a result, He never let the enemy hold Him back from doing the Father's work, and neither should we. If the Lord has given you a work to accomplish, you can expect Him to enable you to navigate around anything the enemy sends your way. You must not allow yourself to be weighed down and immobilized by the onslaught that comes against you in the spirit. It is merely an attempt at intimidation, and you need to exert a little effort and break through enemy lines.

Do not be burdened with the responsibility of constantly battling against the enemy. He merely wants you to get your eyes off the Lord and onto your problems in an attempt to hinder you. It makes him the center of attention.

A good demonstration of this occurred when Nehemiah rebuilt Jerusalem's wall. The men built the wall, but they also had their weapons near them. If war came their way, they were expected to fight, but otherwise they worked. "And it came to pass from that time forth, that the half of my servants wrought in the work, and the other half of them held both the spears, the shields, and the bows, and the habergeons; and the rulers were behind all the house of Judah. They which builded on the wall, and they that bare burdens, with those that laded, every one with one of his hands wrought in the work, and with the other hand held a weapon" (Neh. 4:16–17).

They did not let the opposition stop or slow their progress. In fact, they finished in record time—fifty-two days. Consequently, their enemies realized that the Lord was on their side. "So the wall was finished in the twenty and fifth day of the month Elul, in fifty and two days. And it came to pass, that when all our enemies heard thereof, and all the heathen that were about us saw these things, they were much cast down in their own eyes: for they perceived that this work was wrought of our God" (Neh. 6:15–16).

We have no excuse for not getting the work of the Lord done just because we are under attack. When warfare comes in, do what is necessary and then get back to work. It is a sign of spiritual maturity when you maintain your responsibilities despite the difficulties surrounding you.

Not only that, but Scripture says that when a man's ways please the Lord, He makes his enemies to be at peace with him. If we do not complete the work the Lord has told us to do, how are we ever going to please Him? Pressing past the opposition and completing the work of the Lord is definitely one of the ways to defeat Jezebel in your midst. This builds tenacity and determination in you. You'll always have opposition, but if you learn to press past Jezebel, *nothing* will be able to deter you.

There are, however, days of unusually heavy warfare where an all-out campaign may be launched against you. But, stand. This is a warfare tactic in and of itself. Being immovable when your enemy is trying to move you is victory! If his objective was to move you and you didn't move, then you won that battle.

There is more to warring in the spirit than binding and loosing. The above points may not *appear* to be major, but if this is how the enemy has been causing damage and you just tightened your defenses, then it is major!

# CHAPTER 15—Take Your Rightful Stance

Because you have been up against this principality for a while, it is possible that you are not taking the right stance against the enemy. Initially, when you first encountered Jezebel, the spirit of fear associated with it *may* have been frightening, but after you gained some spiritual muscles, it probably offered no problem.

Nevertheless, it can now operate on a lower level and is not easily detected when other areas of warfare are dominating the scene. As a result, you go after the heavy artillery and ignore the spirit of intimidation that lingers in the background. This robs you, however, of your effectiveness in the Holy Spirit.

Not only that, but you need to have the attitude that you are in charge of the entire scene. If a spirit of intimidation is still in the arena, then you are not taking your rightful stance. It makes you feel like there is a need for constant warfare. This impression comes because the enemy is hitting your "feeling realm" in hopes of suggesting that he is still raging after you have bound him.

Between these two tactics, you are buying into the suggestion that things are not subdued after warring or that your victories are short-lived. This is a lie. When you bind something, it is bound, and he cannot undo it. You need to believe *that* instead of the impressions that you pick up from the enemy's camp.

When you bind Jezebel and the entire company of spirits that accompany it, they truly are bound; however, when the people hosting these spirits begin to pray or make declarations, it is going to feel like they are breaking through. But it only occurs when you drop your shield of faith and doubt the validity of Matthew 16:19. Believe that He has given you the keys of the kingdom and that what you bind is bound and what you loose is loosed. As long as you stand your ground, they can't touch you. You're a child of the Most High God, and based on your union with Christ, you are seated in heavenly places with Him. You have dominion over the enemy, so believe it.

Another tactic of Jezebel is to attempt to penetrate your spirit with intimidation, doubt, and unbelief. Unless you have experienced this, it might sound outrageous. It's not just a case of picking this up in the spirit realm; you can actually sense the enemy trying to lodge itself in your heart. He knows that if he can get you to doubt, your bindings mean nothing. That's how important it is to believe that you're truly binding the enemy!

When you believe you have authority over the enemy as Matthew 16:19 says you do, then your stance against him is correct. Until then, you are not in faith or in full control of the situation. Once you know beyond all doubt that you have authority, he is in trouble, and the battle will turn in your favor permanently. Do not be too quick to boast, "Oh, I know that!" It is one thing to know it and another to live it out in the thick of battle with a principality. However, if you have this truth embedded in your heart, there will be a great peace because he cannot do anything to you. No matter what he throws at you, you *can* overcome in the situation.

This new confidence will also be unsettling to the Jezebelite. Philippians 1:28 says, "And in nothing terrified by your adversaries: which is to them an evident token of perdition, but to you of salvation and that of God." This Scripture usually refers to the enemy, but the principle is the same with people. If you truly have faith in the fact that you possess the keys (or authority) of the kingdom, they will not know what to do. That does not mean the battle stops, but if you maintain your stance and do not get rattled, the victory is yours!

> *When you **know** you have the victory, fear and insecurity will evaporate, and you'll appear more relaxed.*

When you *know* you have victory, fear and insecurity will seem to evaporate, and you will take on a more relaxed appearance. When the oppression has lifted, you no longer project a critical and judgmental attitude. Now that you have the correct stance, the tables are turned. Before, the enemy had intimidated you and you felt boxed in; now there's a reversal.

Consequently, it enables you to respond in love. Before, you were so battle-conscious and uptight that responding graciously to the Jezebelite was next to impossible. Now that you are not threatened, it is easier to love your brethren.

Once you grasp the reality of your authority in the Spirit, your entire demeanor takes on a more Christlike appearance. Before, you may have wanted to appear this way, but when you are taking a pounding, it is hard to come across lovingly.

# CHAPTER 16—Intercession: The Father's Heart

Though we do have the responsibility to war against this principality, we also need to consider the Jezebelite, who is comprised of two parts: a principality operating out of the person's soul realm and a person facing eternity. The Lord often allows us to see His heart toward the Jezebelite so that we will intercede.

Many preach that all you need to do is just love the Jezebelite. This couldn't be further from the truth. Falling all over someone and letting your guard down does not set a church free. In fact, it is possible to be seduced and come under the influence of this spirit yourself. However, there is a safe way to set this captive free.

In Isaiah 59, the Lord says He saw that there was no man and wondered why there was no intercessor. Ezekiel 22:30 says, "And I sought for a man among them, that should make up the hedge and stand in the gap before me for the land, *that I should not destroy it"* (emphasis added).

The Lord does not take pleasure in striking down individuals who wreak havoc upon the body of Christ. He's looking for those who will cry out on their behalf. Satan has gotten a hold of their lives, and they need deliverance. There may be some corrections that will go forth, but it'll be done to reverse their state and return them to the Lord. Sometimes their sin is so grievous that it calls for severe punishment, but the Lord is looking for those who will call for mercy.

In 1 Samuel 7, the children of Israel had been worshipping the gods of Ashtaroth and Baal, which were the same gods worshipped by Jezebel in the time of Elijah. Yet in verse 9, "Samuel took a sucking lamb, and offered it for a burnt offering wholly unto the Lord and cried unto the Lord for Israel and the Lord heard him" and delivered them from their enemies.

There is a reason why Samuel did what he did in chapter 7. We have a hedge of protection around us because of the righteousness of the Lord, but when it is broken down because of sin, there is a gap for the enemy to enter in and destroy us. Here Samuel built up the hedge by asking for Israel's forgiveness through the burnt offering. As a result, their attackers were promptly defeated.

We need to do the same thing for the Jezebelites. Their hedges are broken down because of their sin, and if no one intercedes, rest assured, the enemy will turn on them at some point and utterly destroy them.

We may not *feel* they deserve this mercy, but this is how the Lord operates, and we are to walk in His ways. We build up the hedge for them by asking for their forgiveness. Remember, John 20:23 says that those sins that we remit are remitted. We have the ability to set this captive free.

> *Very often, people with a Jezebel spirit, have been hurt and hide a poor self-image.*

Note that when we stand in the gap to close the opening so the enemy cannot attack them, we ourselves must be righteous. We have to pray them through just like we would an unsaved loved one. Very often people open up to this principality because they have hurts and poor self-images. Jezebelites have an air of superiority and try to control situations, but in actuality, many feel inferior and are fearful of being hurt again. You might argue, "This Jezebelite just about killed me. Let them get what they deserve." But that's not the heart of the Father.

A father's heart consists of mercy, and rarely does a good man give his children what they really deserve. Rather, the discipline is designed to turn them around so they do what is right. After all, our heavenly Father is full of compassion, and it saddens Him when no one cries out to stay His hand of judgment. We have to remember that often these Jezebelites are His wayward children, and His heart breaks for them as they fall deeper and deeper into sin.

The Father looks for us to line up with Him and have His heart of compassion. This is truly a work of grace for some of us who have suffered greatly, but remember, He has allowed this principality to exist so that it would do a work in us. We need to look at this as an opportunity to come up a few levels and become more like Him. How pleasing it would be to Him if we carried out the desires of His heart and lined up with *His* way of doing things. Demanding a just sentence denotes a lower level of understanding and a less mature walk with the Father.

Have you ever thought that the Lord may be waiting for you to cry out in intercession before He releases you from this trial? In Job 42:10, the Lord turned the captivity of Job when he prayed for his friends; also, He gave Job twice as much as he had before. You may have been raked over the coals by the Jezebelite, but there needs to be a transformation in you that only comes because of compassionate intercession.

People need to be set free. If you just run them out of the church, you risk infecting other congregations, and you have no guarantee that you'll be free from retaliation in the spirit at a later date. However, when you pray for their deliverance, you touch the heart of the Lord, you set the Jezebelite free, *and* the enemy is totally defeated.

# CHAPTER 17—Warfare

When you gain ground in the spirit, a Jezebelite will feel threatened and operate as a goddess of war against you. This is a common reaction, so you must learn how to respond correctly. If not, you will be trampled and never make any headway.

When an all-out attack is launched against you in warfare, it is different from having some foul thing sent to you in the spirit realm or finding yourself bound. It can come because of a demonic "intercessory" tongue, or it can just flow out of the Jezebelite, depending on the level of vehemence within. The latter can occur in the solitude of the Jezebelite's heart without any outward visible signs.

When this happens, you will experience intensity in the spirit realm, and your teeth will feel like they are on edge. You will probably be aggravated for seemingly no apparent reason, and your reactions to others may register this.

Along with the attack may come a strong desire to feed your flesh. There will be little or no desire to do anything spiritual, or natural, for that matter. It is a time of temptation, and you will want to yield to those weak areas, primarily because your spirit man is under siege and suddenly your flesh is starting to gain the upper hand.

Feeling terrible, you may be tempted to pamper yourself. *What you really need to do is feed your spirit man, because that is the only thing that will remedy the situation.* If you do not, this flesh-feeding will continue until you are miles away from the Lord, down in the dumps and completely defeated. This, of course, was the strategy intended.

*When warfare hits, it's possible to turn the situation around by sowing in the spirit immediately.*

Instead, start sowing in the Spirit as soon as possible by warring in tongues or singing praise until you feel a release. *It is possible to turn the situation completely around in a short time if you sow to the spirit immediately.* Whatever you do, stay away from those pitfalls that you know will feed your flesh.

This takes great discipline and determination, but think of the negative ramifications if you make concessions to your flesh. It has a bearing on your friends and loved ones. When the enemy attacks, he hits not only you but also your support system. You are a threat to him, and he has to conquer you and those who serve to help you.

During times of warfare, you will notice that the weak within your family will be particularly vulnerable to attack. When you are strong, your prayers cover them, but when you have been knocked out of commission, your shield is down and they get pounded.

You have more than you to consider.

# CHAPTER 18—Stealing in the Spirit Realm

The principality of Jezebel is known for robbing things in the spirit. It has already been established that false prophets surrounded this former queen. Matthew 7:15 warns us to beware of false prophets because they come in sheep's clothing, but inwardly they are ravenous wolves. This principality carries with it an insatiable hunger to acquire both natural and spiritual things. The very nature of this enemy seeks to be the dominant figure. Those with it will not allow anyone to reach their level. As a result, there is a lot of theft going on because they must be top dog. This drive to be first overrides any scruples.

It may be that they see you as a threat, as mentioned previously, or they desire your position, relationship, or promise from the Lord. They want what they want, and nothing is going to stand in their way. If they are intercessors, they will know how to press in until they sense the victory and obtain their objective. It is at this point that something has been stolen in the spirit realm. How can you tell? Suddenly relationships are distant, you lack favor, there is an absence of progress, and there is a general feeling that you have been cut out of the loop to the point that you seem invisible within the church.

You, in the meantime, are sitting there innocently, never thinking that you have been bound from head to foot. When you come to the realization, you may be astonished, but remember that they are deceived and view you as the enemy. This insatiable desire to be on the top drives them.

This robber prince is also capable of walking off with your word or promise from the Lord. If you preach a message, prophesy, or testify about a promise of the Lord, those that operate out of a Jezebel spirit may try to impede or negate its fulfillment by binding or claiming it. If you are making progress in your ministry and it is evident to all, then you had better guard it in the spirit realm. An individual who is trying to be number one will not tolerate new ground.

Remember, these individuals must be dominant, and the way they do this is by destroying your progress and keeping you at a reduced state. If they can figure out where you are going, they will attempt to head you off. You may argue that if the Lord gave you a word, then He will fulfill it. Nevertheless, if this is your promise, then it is your responsibility to hold on to it, guard it, and pray until it comes in. Most words are not stolen, so it sounds unusual; but when Jezebel is in your midst, these things do occur.

*When the enemy steals your promise, it feels like the Lord never said a thing, and there's not one ounce of faith left.*

How would you know if the enemy has stolen it? When you get a word from the Lord, He also gives faith, encouragement, and even an excitement in your spirit. There is a sense that the promise actually exists in the spirit realm and is waiting for you to pull it down to the natural realm. However, when the enemy steals your promise, it feels like the Lord never said a thing, and there's not one ounce of faith left.

Do not be naïve, because the enemy will use a Jezebelite to sweep you clean of all that you hold dear. If you testify that the Lord answered a prayer, then you should be on guard because there will be an attempt to steal that which is newly acquired. This way you will not gain any strength, nor will you look better than they do.

It is paramount to know what happens when these stolen goods are taken from you. In the spirit, the enemy confiscates them, so it's important to cut the bonds from the stolen items, and command the enemy to return that which he has taken.

If money is a requirement for successfully fulfilling the Lord's commission, that, too, can be confiscated. It is possible to be operating in the Malachi 3:10 blessing and suddenly find your funds completely dried up and debt creeping in. If you have not had difficulty handling your finances and suddenly you are unable to meet expenses, look no further. It is more than likely that a giant Python spirit has wrapped itself around your finances, or someone is laying claim to your blessing and stealing it in order to hinder your work. Bind the thief, loose your blessings, and command them to return to you.

But fear not; this, too, can be eliminated. There is a problem only when there's no word of knowledge concerning the precise demonic force that is involved. That is why a close and obedient walk with the Lord is necessary when dealing with this principality, because the Lord will withhold information until you are in the correct position. After that, the situation can be easily resolved. The enemy can get away with this only when saints are ignorant of his devices. Once the light exposes his scheme, the game is over; but keep in mind that the Lord will not divulge the necessary information until you are walking correctly.

# CHAPTER 19—Murder for a Vineyard

When Jezebel is in residence within a congregation, many saints may find themselves sick because they have encountered this spirit. Such things merely flow from a Jezebelite if prompted by jealousy or anger. If you are conscious of these possibilities, it does not really pose a problem because you simply bind things periodically and remain alert in the spirit.

*Jezebel actually conducted the death of Naboth in the privacy of her home through sorcery and witchcraft.*

Something else that people need to be aware of is the threat of murder. Before you dismiss the possibility, think of 1 Kings 19 and 21. In both chapters, Jezebel resorts to murder to solve the problem. She certainly threatened Elijah with death because he killed her false prophets, and she acquired Naboth's vineyard with a crafty plot of murder. *Keep in mind that Jezebel actually conducted the death of Naboth in the privacy of her home through sorcery and witchcraft.* She had control over various individuals who carried out her plot. She even made it look like a godly assignment with fasting and prayer and enlisted the support of a spirit of false accusation to make her plot complete. Had we not been told otherwise, she would have looked very innocent to us.

Such is the case with modern-day Jezebelites. Spiritual forces carry out murder behind the scenes as jealousy and revenge flow from the Jezebelites' hearts. Sometimes Jezebelites vocalize the threat of murder and sometimes not. Regardless, it is entirely possible for this spirit to flow, even unwittingly, as situations increase in intensity. The more vehement the "prayers" of Jezebelites become, the greater the chance of this spirit coming into play. The enemy is given the right to do more and more damage as the Jezebelites' hatred or sin increases. Just as the Spirit of the Lord increases as we yield to the Lord and follow His ways, so it is in the kingdom of darkness. There may be other reasons, as mentioned in the chapter on obedience.

Anyone who stands up to a Jezebelite runs the risk of retaliation because a Jezebelite is full of pride and must be the dominant figure. This is done through control, so if an individual does not respond to intimidation, rejection, and an onslaught of trouble, then the ultimate of control must be employed—a spirit of death, destruction, murder, and vendetta. Those involved may or may not be cognizant that this is going forth from them. On the other hand, most targets are unaware of a Jezebel spirit and have no idea how to defend themselves; therefore, they are easy marks because they offer no resistance in the spirit realm where the battle is being fought.

Many leaders do not have discernment, or perhaps their call is in an entirely different area. They may find this hard to swallow; however, if the Lord has opened you up to this area or you have experienced this firsthand, then you know that it is perfectly feasible. Very often the person with the Jezebel spirit will threaten an individual, even with specific details, as a means of intimidation. If the target offers no resistance, it will most assuredly succumb. Keep in mind that Elijah was threatened, but after his initial panic attack, the Lord girded him up. Eventually, however, the Lord turned things around, and Jezebel's death occurred exactly as Elijah had prophesied. With God on your side, all things are possible.

# CHAPTER
## 20—Overcomers!

"Notwithstanding I have a few things against thee, because thou sufferest that woman Jezebel" (Rev 2:20).

The Lord was displeased with the church at Thyatira because they suffered, or allowed, Jezebel to remain in the church. If the truth be known, there are probably a number of individuals who discern Jezebel in their church but choose to look the other way because it can be an intimidating and imposing giant. However, the Scriptures clearly state that we are not to allow this prince to exist within our surroundings.

The purpose of this book was to demonstrate the work of the Lord that can be done in believers' lives when they encounter Jezebel, but there will come a time when the Lord will require you to dethrone this prince. You are not to allow Jezebel to exist in your realm of influence.

When this period of training is complete as mentioned above, you will have the ability to over-throw the principality of Jezebel. After engaging in warfare for a season, you will be able to detect a general overall weakening and realize that the tables have turned. It is important, however, to continue until there is a complete capitulation and this prince is overthrown. People will experience a great release, and God's purposes and plans will become reality in the natural.

It is essential to tear this principality down, for the Lord has clearly given us the authority over the enemy according to numerous Scriptures. "Behold, I give unto you power to tread on serpents and scor-pions, and over all the power of the enemy: and nothing shall by any means hurt you" (Luke 10:19).

*He gives us His authority and His power.* When He says that He has given us the keys of the kingdom (Matt.16:19), they are *His keys.* We need to meditate on this.

He has taken the keys of hell and death from Satan, and He has spoiled him and made a public display of him by triumphing over him. We have this same authority. It is His authority within us based on our union with Him.

Not only are we expected to overthrow this prince, but God greatly rewards those who oppose it. When we pull down Jezebel, the Lord considers us overcomers.

To support this further, we see Jacob as he awaits his brother Esau in Genesis 32. In verses 9 and 12, he reminds the Lord of His promise to deal well with him and make his descendants as numerous as the sands of the sea. Generally, we have all received promises in our lives for which we have to stand in faith. If you have encountered a Jezebel in some individual, you will certainly have to contend with the person for the very promises of God. The enemy does not want you to come into all that the Lord has for you. Therefore, you, like Jacob, will have to contend with God and man.

When we submit to the circumstances created by Jezebel in our midst and act righteously, it is the equivalent of wrestling with the Lord. Each time we come before the Lord to remind Him of His promise, He reminds us of another area of our lives that needs changing. Since one of the main purposes of the Lord is to transform us into His likeness and image, we cannot fault Him for trying to get as much mileage as possible out of this trial.

It was Jacob's tenacity that caused the Lord to give him a new name and his promise. Just like Jacob who wrestled all night, we may go on for years in this transformation mode until we fulfill the requirements of the Lord. This is struggling with the Lord. Genesis 32:25-26 says, "And when he saw that he could not prevail against him, he touched the hollow of his thigh. Let me go for the day breaketh."

Genesis 32:25 can occur toward the end of your trial when a situation arises that is so grievous that you won't feel like going on. Jacob had endured a wrestling match that lasted for hours, and at the very end, the angel dealt him a terrible blow that inflicted great pain. Nevertheless, Jacob was relentless: "I will not let you go until you bless me!"

There may come a time prior to breakthrough when it is so painful that you will want to give up, but this is what it means to overcome. Jacob did not release his hold but insisted on his promise. This speaks volumes about his character. He was tenacious and refused to give up despite the duration or the level of difficulty. As a result, the Lord said in verse 28, "Thy name shall be no more called Jacob, but Israel, for as a prince thou hast power with God and with men and thou hast prevailed. "

"And he that overcometh, and keepeth my works unto the end, to him will I give power over the nations" (Rev 2:24–26). "To him that overcometh will I grant to sit with me in my throne, even as I also overcame, and am set down with my Father in his throne" (Rev 3:21).

The Lord highly esteems the believer who overcomes and completes the entire course. Over the years, the Lord transformed Jacob from a deceiver into someone who was tenacious and determined. Toward the end of his life, he was well respected and known for his good character.

The Father is holy, and we His children are to be like Him. We are not to despise His chastening and look only for His blessing, but we are to allow Him to work His character in our lives. Not only is there satisfaction in our souls as we endure the difficulties, but there's an intimate level of His presence that cannot be obtained otherwise.

*As Americans, we often pull back from suffering and fail to reach the high calling of Christ.*

As Americans, we often pull back from any form of suffering because we live for pleasure. As a result, the Lord is able to complete only a portion of His character within us. Many times He continues to bless us, but we fail to reach the high calling of Christ.

The church of Christ is generally pleasure-oriented instead of character-oriented. However, when we humble ourselves under the mighty hand of God, we are allowing Him to do what is important to Him. He is a God of character, and He desires above all that His children look and act like Him. While it can be difficult at times, the Lord abundantly makes up for any loss with an increase of His intimate presence. He also makes us privy to things that He does not share with those who withdraw from His unusual training. These benefits far outweigh any discomfort, and there will be a deep satisfaction and contentment that materialism will never yield.

Let us run with patience the race that is set before us, looking unto Jesus the author and finisher of our faith; who for the joy that was set before him endured the cross, despising the shame, and is set down at the right hand of the throne of God. For consider him that endured such contradiction of sinners against himself, lest ye be wearied and faint in your minds. Ye have not yet resisted unto blood, striving against sin. And ye have forgotten the exhortation which speaketh unto you as unto children, my son, despise not thou the chastening of the Lord, nor faint when thou art rebuked of him: for whom the Lord loveth he chasteneth, and scourgeth every son whom he receiveth.

Hebrews 12:1-6

If Jezebel is in your midst, choose to yield to the chastening or instruction of the Lord, and let Him build His character in you. Downplay Jezebel, and just allow Him to qualify you for the company of Elijahs that will usher in His second coming!

Come, Lord Jesus! Come!

# BIBLIOGRAPHY

Clark, Jonas. *Exposing Spiritual Witchcraft.* Hallandale, Florida: Spirit of Life Ministries, 1995.

Ing, Richard. *Spiritual Warfare.* New Kensington, Pennsylvania: Whitaker House, 1996.

Sheets, Dutch. *Watchman Prayer: How to Stand Guard and Protect Your Family, Home and Community.* Ventura, California: Regal, 2000.

Swindoll, Charles. *Elijah: A Man of Heroism and Humility.* Nashville, Tennessee: W Publishing, 2000.

# Various Demonic Categories or Topics Under Jezebel

| | | |
|---|---|---|
| Fear | Dividing | Wrong Prayers |
| Trepidation | Divorcing | Wrong Anointing |
| Intimidation | Separating | Wrong Declarations |
| Alarm | Setting Apart | |
| Panic | Setting Against | Blocks |
| Fright | Indifference | Bondages |
| Worry | | Incapacitations |
| Fretting | Troublemaking | |

| | | |
|---|---|---|
| Doubt | Force of Feuding | Impediment |
| Unbelief | Alienation | Hindrance |
| Anxiety | Cutting | Obstruction |
| Nervousness | Hostility | Interference |
| | | Sabotage |
| Infirmity | Discrediting | |
| Affliction | Undermining | Defeat |
| Lying Symptoms | Undercutting | Discouragement |
| Pain & Torment | False Accusations | Depression |
| | | Despair |
| Mind Control | Extermination | Despondency |
| Tentacles | Eradication | Despondency |
| Giant Squid | Annihilation | Suicide |
| Bands on the Head | Destruction | Self-Pity |
| Confusion | Dissemination of Will | |
| Vain Imagination | | Jealousy |
| Rumination | Death | Pride |

| | | |
|---|---|---|
| Distraction | Destruction | Seeking Supremacy |
| Obfuscation | Murder | Showmanship |
| | Vendetta | Up-One-Manship |
| Jezebel | | |
| Leviathon | Witchcraft | Drawing |
| Python | Sorcery | Swaying |
| | | Enlisting |
| Goddess of War | Siren Spirit | Beguiling |
| | | Seducing |
| Satanic Suspicions | Satanic Perceptions | |
| Suggestions | Projections | |
| Impressions | | |
| Illusions | | |

CPSIA information can be obtained at www.ICGtesting.com
Printed in the USA
268794BV00001B/37/A